STEAM LION

STEAM LION

A BIOGRAPHY OF SAMUEL CUNARD

JOHN G. LANGLEY

BRICK
TOWER
PRESS

Brick Tower Press

© John G. Langley

Published in the United States by Brick Tower Press and
simultaneously in Canada by Nimbus Publishing, Ltd.

Langley, John G.
Steam Lion, A Biography of Samuel Cunard
Foreword by Commodore R. W. Warwick

I. Cunard, Sir Samuel, 1787-1865   2. Maritime
History–Canadian–Biography 3. Economic History-Commerce

ISBN 1-883283-50-7, First US Edition, December 2006
ISBN13 978-1-883283-50-6

Library of Congress
       Control Number: 2006933839

Printed in Canada

To Douglas Logan Gordon — a Cunarder.

TABLE OF CONTENTS

FOREWORD

F ew companies in the world today can lay claim to as rich a history as the Cunard Line can. The Line, as we know it, was established in 1839 to bridge the North Atlantic with a fleet of steamships delivering the mail. To this day, over 166 years later, those early visions of its founder are still in existence, albeit in a slightly different form. Although the Cunard Line moved on from family leadership in the 1920s, the standards set by the family have continued. The company's owners, shore-based executives, and even the most junior members of the shipboard staff have all inherited the will and determination to ensure the company continues to succeed. At times, the future of the company has seemed in doubt, particularly in the mid-1990s. Fortunately, the fragmented ownership and management of those years was not unnoticed by the Carnival Corporation, which now owns the Cunard Line. Under the leadership of the Arisons, a family that shares similar visions to those of Samuel Cunard, the company has grown from strength to strength and remained a dominant force on the North Atlantic.

Since the early days of paddle steamers, maritime technology has continuously advanced, culminating in 2003 with the largest, most technologically advanced passenger liner ever to be built, the *Queen Mary 2*. This book, however, is not about Cunard's liners, but about the man that set the company on its immensely successful course.

This book will navigate you through the life of the Cunard family and its contribution to commerce in Canada long before the *Britannia* sailed from Liverpool on the July 4, 1840, on its historic first voyage. You will read of early ventures with house building, forestry, real estate, community affairs, sailing ships, China tea, mining, and shipbuilding, to name just a few of the numerous enterprises associated with Samuel Cunard. As we await the delivery in 2007 of the Cunard

Line's newest addition to the fleet, the *Queen Victoria*, it is fitting that we are able to acknowledge the achievements of the company's founder.

I am honoured and proud to have been asked to command the *Queen Mary 2*, but those who know me are aware that one of the joys of the position is my association with the long maritime history of the Cunard Line. As a serving seafarer with the line, my deep respect and gratitude goes to John G. Langley for recording the life of this great man, part of whose legacy has been the majority of my seafaring career and life, not to mention those of my father, mother, brother, and nephew, who have all served with the Cunard Line.

This volume is a great tribute to Cunard, and there is no one better to relate this history than John, whose passion inspired him to become the founding director and chairman of the Cunard Steamship Society, dedicated to the preservation of Cunard history. John was instrumental in Canada Post's commemoration of Sir Samuel Cunard in 2004, the placement of his portrait on a postage stamp, thus leading to renewed interest in the Cunard dynasty and the much-anticipated unveiling of a statue of Cunard in Halifax in October 2006. On behalf of present and future generations, my sincere thanks go to John, for all he has done to give Sir Samuel Cunard this very special honour in Canadian history.

Commodore R. W. Warwick
At Sea, March 2006

PREFACE

September 25, 2004, was a picture-perfect day in Halifax, Nova Scotia. The sun rose into a cloudless azure blue sky over Halifax Harbour, and seagulls were the only things moving across the still water.

As the sun began to warm the air, people gathered along the harbourfront. Soon there were thousands, standing three and four deep along the water. Looking seaward, they waited. As if on cue, the *Queen Mary 2*, the newly minted flagship of the Cunard Line, steamed into the harbour. This was no ordinary call. The *Queen Mary 2* was the first true ocean liner to be built since the 1967 launch of the *Queen Elizabeth 2* — nearly four decades ago. September 25, 2004, was the new ship's inaugural visit to Halifax, the home of company founder Samuel Cunard.

Under the command of Commodore Ronald W. Warwick, the ship proceeded without the aid of tugs to Pier 21, Canada's immigration gateway and home to many of the great Cunarders of the past. The spirit of Samuel Cunard was very much alive in the city of his birth.

I have been asked many times how I acquired such an interest in Samuel Cunard. There is no simple explanation. I have always had a natural inclination towards ships and the sea — probably because I have "salt in the blood," a characteristic common to most Maritimers. I, like Samuel Cunard, proudly claim Halifax as my birthplace. Having ancestors who made their livelihood as masters and shipwrights during the twilight of Nova Scotia's Age of Sail has probably also influenced me. Those who believe in fate might attribute my predilection to the fact that as a youth I lived for a while in what had been, years earlier, a Cunard property known as Emscote, though I only learned of Cunard's connection to that South End Halifax house years later, when I was already a Cunard historian. Another peculiar coincidence occurred in the late 1980s, when my wife and I purchased property in Baddeck, Nova Scotia, that we later discovered had belonged to James Duffus, Samuel Cunard's brother-in-law.

As remarkable as these coincidences may be, the reason I wrote this book is to acquaint the reader with the personality of one of Nova Scotia's greatest native sons. Cunard was a Haligonian who rose to prominence as a Maritime entrepreneur and who, by the time of his death in 1865, had attained international stature as the "colonial" who succeeded in bridging the North Atlantic with steam.

There have been many books written about the Cunard Line, the achievement for which Samuel Cunard is best remembered; the company has a fascinating and remarkable history. Many of these works devote a chapter or two to some aspects of Cunard's early years, but there have been few efforts to write a biography of the man. This is an attempt to do just that. I by no means claim this to be a definitive work—there is more to be written, and I hope that others will accept the challenge to write about his life.

Not many people know that Cunard was a Nova Scotian or that he spent most of his life in his native Halifax, where, as head of the venerable firm S. Cunard and Company, he rose to prominence and became a Maritime merchant prince. The first half of the nineteenth century was a formative time in the commercial and social development of Halifax and the Maritime Provinces, and Samuel Cunard played a prominent role in the mercantile community in that era. By learning about his life, the first fifty years of which were spent in Halifax, I hope the reader will gain an appreciation of our own history and, through it, understand how Cunard attained such success as founder of the Cunard—a line that continues to thrive, as evidenced by the magnificent *Queen Mary 2*.

John G. Langley
Baddeck, Nova Scotia, July 2006

July 21, 1840 — Boston Harbour is thrumming with politicians, businesspeople, civic leaders, members of the judiciary, and the public at large. The city is ready for a celebration, and its citizens are waiting impatiently for the arrival of a new age.

The *Britannia* finally enters the harbour loaded with the mail from England, ushering in the Age of Steam to the Atlantic. Samuel Cunard's vision is realized. The world is never the same.

CHAPTER 1

COMING TO AMERICA

To understand how Samuel Cunard became a pioneer of the North Atlantic, it's helpful to look at his ancestors, who were pioneers in America. Samuel Cunard's ancestors were Quakers of German descent. His great-great-grandfather was Thones M. Kunders, a prosperous dyer in Krefeld, Germany, a town on the Lower Rhine near Düsseldorf and the Dutch frontier. Kunders and his wife Helene were Quakers, members of the Society of Friends founded by George Fox in 1648 and devoted to peace, plainness of dress, simplicity of speech, and religious freedom.

The Kunderses and twelve other families from Krefeld immigrated to America in 1683. Thirty-three Krefelders, most of whom were related, settled in the area that would later become Philadelphia, the cradle of American democracy and civil liberty. They were part of the first group of mass immigrants to America and their story is tied to that of the famous Quaker and founder of Pennsylvania, William Penn.

William Penn was born in England on October 14, 1644. His parents, Margaret Jasper and Sir William Penn, Admiral of the British Fleet, were Anglicans. Although a member of the landed gentry by birth, young William Penn was soon to take on a character and personality quite unlike that of his own father. His early life was somewhat unremarkable. He learned law at Lincoln's Inn, studied at the Huguenot Academy at Saumer. However, he soon demonstrated some radical thinking that saw him expelled from Oxford and led to his conversion to Quakerism as a result of the influence of the apostle Thomas Loe.

William Penn found Quakerism a good vehicle for the expression of his own humanitarian and religious beliefs. The Quaker movement, the Society of Friends, endorsed pacificism and refused to bow to the authority of the king. Young Penn was arrested on many occasions and imprisoned in the Tower of London for his radical preachings. In 1677 he moved with his wife, Gulielma Springett, to Holland, accompanied by fellow Quaker George Fox, hoping to turn his ideals into action. In England, meanwhile, the Admiral's son had become an embarrassment to his father; the Quaker cause advocated by William was a nuisance to king and country.

By 1681 King Charles II owed a sizable personal debt to Admiral William Penn, who was rebuilding the British Navy for war with the Dutch. All the while, son William was busy putting his radical thoughts to paper. He soon wrote a charter for a group of Quaker colonists in New Jersey, entitled "Concessions and Agreements." The charter addressed a number of fundamental rights and freedoms, including the right to trial by jury and freedom from arbitrary imprisonment for debt, as well as a fiat denouncing capital punishment. American historians would later describe this document as "the first clear statement of the supremacy of the fundamental law [universal rights] over any statutes that might be enacted." The stage was set for the renegade son to give form and substance to his own beliefs.

Penn, seeing the success of the Quaker pioneers in New Jersey, saw opportunity in America for himself and his group. Although a Quaker himself, his well-to-do upbringing led Penn to be somewhat extravagant. He lived beyond his means, and in the process, incurred personal debt of his own. With a certain shrewdness that perhaps was hereditary, William saw an opportunity to raise capital and at the same time promote and practice his religious beliefs. He had long since become convinced that religious freedom couldn't be achieved in England. Opportunity awaited in the New World, in America.

In one of history's greatest "accommodations," William, aware of the debt owed by King Charles II to Admiral Penn, arranged through his father to "call in" this debt. Seeing a way to rid the kingdom of the troublesome Quakers and at the same time discharge his indebtedness to his admiral, the King, on March 4, 1681, granted William Penn a charter in America for territory northwest of the Delaware River and north of Maryland, later to become Pennsylvania. From a practical perspective, Penn hoped to raise capital by selling tracts of the new territory to settlers and thus clear his own debt, but more importantly, he saw the charter as an opportunity to carry out a "holy experiment." This experiment would become the "seed of the nation," where "free, sober and industrious" people would live in peace and harmony according to their own laws. It wasn't in Penn's mind to call the colony after himself; he wanted to call it New Wales or Sylvania. However, King Charles II proposed and eventually prevailed with the name Pennsylvania, named after Admiral Penn, by then deceased.

William wanted his colony to be an asylum for those fleeing religious persecution, and an environment of freedom and equality — principles that would be equated with what would come to be known as the American Dream. In his search for candidates to inhabit his new world, Penn chose righteous, pious, God-fearing men and their families to fulfill his dream of a land where people were free to worship without fear of retribution. On the lower River Rhine, in the town of Krefeld, Germany, Penn found thirteen families, thirty-three souls who, preferring God's wilderness to men's wars, were prepared to divest themselves of business and property for the unknown virgin wilderness of America.

On July 24, 1683, Thones and Helene Kunders and their three sons were one of the original thirteen families to embark at London for America aboard the five-hundred-ton British schooner *Concord*, with William Jeffries as master. They would arrive some seventy-five days later and settle a place they named Germantown, six miles distant from the future city of Philadelphia. The families drew lots for equal shares in the six thousand acres granted to them by William Penn. Before departing Krefeld, Thones Kunders had astutely purchased a warrant for a further five hundred acres.

The land they settled upon was a fertile but stark wilderness. Life at first was extremely difficult. Winter was upon the families soon after they disembarked from the *Concord*. They arranged to dig cellars, which were covered over and which formed their shelters for their first American winter, a particularly harsh one for the Krefelders. The settlers built their first permanent homes of logs and later of local stone. They raised flax, built looms, and set up spinning wheels. Many were accustomed to growing grapes, so when they saw wild grapes they established their own vineyards. Krefeld was noted for its manufacturers of silk, linen, and other woven goods, talents that these German settlers brought with them to America. The great carpet and other textile-related industries of Pennsylvania as well as America's publishing houses and newspapers may be said to have originated from early beginnings in Germantown. The official seal of Germantown bears at its centre a trifolium, having a grape vine on one leaf, flax blossoms on another, and a weaver's spool on a third, with the inscription *Vinum, Linum et Textrinum*. The Germantown Fair, first held in 1701, became a centre for exhibiting and selling the products of these craftspeople.

By diligent industry, Thones and Helene Kunders persisted, and slowly their farm showed signs of modest prosperity. More immigrants arrived, and by the late 1600s, Germantown had grown around a main street bordered by peach trees and anchored by a central market. Following Penn's suggestion, the settlers had chosen not to reside on scattered farms, but followed the European pattern of living together in a town. Germantown fast became the earliest example of urban planning in America. More than fifty families built spacious farm buildings and tended their three-acre town plots, growing vegetables and flowers. The fields of the town lay north and south. Led by the Krefelders, the German settlers, with a love and respect for the land, actively practiced stewardship principles that would be the envy of conservationists today. In addition to working the land, the colonists continued in their trade of weaving and dyeing materials described as "very fine German linens such as no person of quality need be ashamed to wear."

It wasn't long before Thones Kunders began to play a leading role in the community. Germantown was incorporated in 1689; Kunders became mayor in 1691. His home was large enough to be used as a temporary meeting place for the Friends to worship until their first formal Meeting House was built. He served as recorder of the courts and as a juryman. He was one of the signatories to the first resolution against slavery in America. In Proud's *History of Pennsylvania*, Thones Kunders is described as "an hospitable well-disposed man, of an inoffensive lifestyle and good character."

Thones Kunders died in 1729 at the age of ninety-six. He had spent the last forty-six years of his life in America. In addition to the three German-born sons who immigrated to America with them, Thones and Helene had four more children born in Germantown, including three daughters — Ann, Agnes, and Elizabeth — and a son, Henry, born in 1688. During his lifetime, Thones Kunders was also known as Dennis Cunrads, and over the years the family surname took on many variations in spelling, including Conard, Conders, Conrad, Cunnard, Cunrade, Cunrads, Cunraeds, Kunders, and Cunard.

Katherine Streypers was the daughter of one of the other thirteen families to settle Germantown. She and Henry Cunrad (the variant he chose) married on June 28, 1710, and shortly after moved to a farm in nearby Whitpain Township, Montgomery County. The Quakers of Germantown recommended Henry and Katherine to the people of Whitpain as "both of a sober and honest disposition." There the two prospered and had seven sons, the youngest of whom was named Samuel. Some of the second-generation American Kunderses assumed the surname "Conrad"; others, including Samuel, chose the name "Cunard," the surname that Samuel's second son, Abraham, would take with him to Nova Scotia in the great Loyalist Emigration of 1783.

The first Krefeld families found America to be a haven of peace and tolerance. For some of their grandchildren, however, it was fast becoming a land divided between loyalty to the king or to the colonies. Suspicion and persecution were commonplace. Prior to 1775, loyalty to the king and a desire to preserve connection with Britain were not frowned upon, but from the autumn of 1776, just after the Declaration of Independence was adopted, until the autumn of 1783, New York and Long Island were essentially the only safe place of refuge for those who chose to remain loyal to the Crown and King George III. Among the thirty thousand Loyalists gathered behind the British lines were two grandsons of Henry Cunrad — Abraham, as yet unmarried, and his cousin Robert, with his wife and young son. They were the only descendants of Thones Kunders to remain loyal to the King. When the American Revolution was over and the expulsion of Loyalists began, they lost everything — their homes, properties, and businesses. Just one hundred years after their ancestors had set sail from Germany, Abraham and Robert departed — were deported, in fact — with the British fleet for Nova Scotia.

On November 30, 1782, Article Seven of the Peace Treaty stipulated that "his Britannic Majesty shall with all convenient speed and without causing any destruction, or carrying of Negroes or other property of the American inhabitants, withdraw all his armies, garrisons and fleets from the said United States." Accordingly, on April 23, 1783, a convoy of thirty-two ships, dubbed the Spring Fleet, was assembled from various ports on Long Island and New York. It sailed from Sandy Hook three days later, bound for Port Roseway, Annapolis Royal, Halifax, and other ports in Nova Scotia, as well as the St. John River and Fort Cumberland. The ship carrying the Cunards was the *Union*, with Captain Wilson as master. It was a vessel of 287 tons and it transported 164 passengers. Among them was Thomas Murphy, a wealthy shipbuilder from South Carolina, whose tall, dark-eyed daughter, Margaret, caught the eye of Abraham Cunard. A shipboard romance soon blossomed.

The *Union* made its way north to the Bay of Fundy, landing at Parrtown, later to become Saint John—the Loyalist City in New Brunswick. There Robert and his family disembarked and settled upon their land grant, lot 1008. Abraham Cunard and the Murphys decided to go on to Halifax, the garrison town on the east coast of Nova Scotia. There Abraham would receive and settle on a grant of a shore lot on the Halifax waterfront. The Murphys would eventually continue to the township of Rawdon, some forty miles distant from Halifax, and settle upon a grant provided to Thomas Murphy as one of a number of Loyalists from South Carolina who had served for a short time under Lord Rawdon during the revolutionary war.

Halifax was essentially a town founded for war. Established in 1749 as a British military stronghold to offset the threat of the French at Louisbourg, it was built on the site of a rocky hill, its highest point being commanded by a strong fortress called the Citadel. A stockade was erected around the landward side of the town and augmented by five forts. Streets were set out and over two hundred houses were built that first year, primarily of wood from the surrounding forests. From its crude beginnings, hastily constructed to protect its settlers, the town grew and the Royal Navy Dockyard was established in 1757, with all the conveniences for the handling, victualling, and repairing of the largest ships of His Majesty's Navy. Halifax was the rendezvous point for the British fleet and army before and after the siege of Quebec. In preparation for the coming attack on the Fortress of Louisbourg, the town experienced a new incursion with the arrival of eleven battalions of British Redcoats, two battalions of the Royal American Regiment, and a corps of Rogers' Rangers. All these troops, numbering in excess of twelve thousand, were encamped on the slopes of Citadel Hill and to the west of what came to be called Camp Hill.

In the ensuing years, Louisbourg was held by both the French and the English, before the final defeat of the French in 1758. The declining French influence in North America ushered in a time of peace and prosperity. The blood and terror of war died away and a new tide of immigration from New England moved north to Nova Scotia. Lots in Halifax were selling for fifty guineas at the time. Many new buildings were erected in the town, some with stone and hardware from the shattered fortress at Louisbourg. A place was cleared for a public hospital and a school building commenced for orphaned children. The frame for St. Paul's Church, which had been brought from Boston, was erected and covered. A brick manufacturing plant commenced construction. The garrison town was taking on form and substance.

The coming of the Loyalists to Nova Scotia in 1783 was a pivotal event in the colony's history. In terms of numbers, this mass migration to its shores was the equivalent of the Norman invasion of England in 1066. At the time, Nova Scotia included all of New Brunswick, Saint John's Island (Prince Edward Island), and Cape Breton. The fleets pouring into Nova Scotia disembarked ten times more Loyalists than there were existing colonists. The local population was swamped by a transplanted population of some thirty-four thousand Loyalists. Among them were English, Scots, Irish, Hessians, Prussians, French, Swiss, Dutch, and Germans. There was also a sizable contingent of blacks, some freed slaves and soldiers from the Black Pioneer Battalion and some who were still slaves, travelling with their masters.

The Halifax in which Abraham Cunard found himself was a struggling, wooden town defended by the tumbled remains of forts thrown up or repaired for the American Revolution. In the eyes of some Loyalists from Boston, it was "a miserable village in which most of the houses were in a dilapidated state, letting in the bleak winds of the season through manifold chinks, hardly a room ever known the luxury of being plastered."

Many of the Loyalists who disembarked at Halifax in 1783 were in a destitute and helpless condition. The town was unable to house them properly, and tent encampments were hastily erected on the slopes of Citadel Hill, on the Halifax Commons, and in the woods at Point Pleasant Park. Public buildings, warehouses, and churches had been turned into temporary shelters. Private accommodation was at a premium. Stores, sheds, and cook stoves were brought up from the ships and set up in the streets. There was no sewage. Local dung patrols were established to clean the privies out into wheelbarrows, which were dumped into the harbour. Filth accumulated and remained in the streets until the rain washed it away. The soil around the town was rocky and largely unsuitable for farming. Fresh food was available only during the short summer season; salt meat and fish were the staple items, along with bread and potatoes. This limited diet caused widespread sickness, particularly scurvy. Smallpox was very common, and the graveyards received far too many people before their time.

Although physical and emotional hardship was the lot of most early Halifax settlers, there was much that was positive. While in New York, the Loyalists had signed Articles of Settlement, which, among other things, promised them provisions for two years, a grant of land, and a quantity of boards and shingles with which to erect habitation.

Abraham Cunard was given his choice of several different lots, and, attracted to the water, he claimed a shore lot in an undeveloped area between the town and the dockyard. The lot ran up the hill from the harbour to a muddy lane later to be named Brunswick Street. Near the top of the hill, not far from a little church built by German settlers, Abraham built himself a modest two-storey house of squared timber. His skill as a carpenter enabled him to find a job with the Royal Navy Dockyard soon after he arrived in Halifax. Always his thoughts dwelt upon the spirited, dark-eyed girl he had met aboard the ship that had brought them to Halifax. Margaret Murphy, settled with her parents in Rawdon, was a tough five-hour horseback ride through woods and hills away. Still, when his house was completed, Abraham went to court his love.

CHAPTER 2

THE EARLY YEARS

Samuel Cunard was born in a small cottage on a hillside over-looking the harbour in Halifax, Nova Scotia on Thursday, November 21, 1787. He was the second of nine children of Abraham and Margaret (Murphy) Cunard, who had settled in an area off Brunswick Street, just to the north and outside the perimeter of the Halifax Citadel. The site was thoughtfully chosen, close as it was to the Royal Navy Dockyard, where Abraham secured employment and would later rise to the position of master carpenter. The Cunards' first child, Mary, was born the year after they were married; their last child was born in 1804. Such a large family — seven sons (Samuel, William, Joseph, John, Thomas, Henry, and Edward) and two daughters (Mary and Susan) — was not uncommon for this time.

Samuel was born with salt in his veins. His first breath was of the briny sea air that permeated the harbour just a stone's throw from his birthplace. Halifax was little changed from the garrison town his parents had arrived in a few years earlier. There was talk of war between Britain and France; the French Foreign Office had recalled diplomats and military personnel from England, and in Britain, army and navy officers and ratings were being brought back to active duty, and press gangs were busy conscripting the unwary and the unwilling into the service of His Majesty.

From his bedroom window overlooking the waterfront, young Samuel was a spectator to the seafaring world. Here merchant ships and men-of-war swung at anchor or tied up at one of the many wharves that reached out from the shores of Halifax's magnificent ice-free harbour. The Royal Navy Dockyard was located just to the north of the Cunard property. Samuel's earliest memories were the sights and sounds of the waterfront. Almost daily he would have awoken to see a forest of different-sized masts. His other senses would have taken in the smell of hemp, oakum, tar, and drying canvas, and the sounds of block and tackle, the hammer, the adze, the blacksmith's anvil, and always the living sounds of the vessels themselves as they creaked and groaned with the movement of the water beneath their keels. No vessels entering the harbour caused greater interest than packet boats arriving from England. They brought the mails and newspapers containing news from Europe and the outside world, which was quickly reproduced in the local weekly newspapers.

By the time Samuel was ten years of age, his father had methodically acquired various plots of land running east and downhill to the water's edge from Brunswick Street. In 1796 Abraham purchased for five hundred pounds the nucleus of what would become the Cunard commercial empire. This comprised Lot Seventeen in the North Suburbs, a parcel that included waterfrontage and a wharf. He would go on to secure titles to other adjoining real estate and water lots, making Samuel Cunard's playground like few others. He soon learned his way around the waterfront and it was not long before he engaged in his first business initiative: gathering up remnants from broken lots of dry goods and packaging and reselling them at a profit. The Halifax piers were his training grounds; the experience he gained there would shape his character.

Samuel received his early formal education at the Halifax Grammar School, which had been established in 1789 in a building where the legislative assembly met, at the corner of Barrington and Sackville streets. When Samuel became a student, the Reverend George Wright, a graduate of Trinity College, Dublin, was headmaster. Wright had moved to the New England colonies early in his life. After the American Revolution, he came to Halifax, where he served for many years both as headmaster of the grammar school and, from 1799 to his death in 1819, as minister of St. George's Round Church.

The education obtained by Samuel Cunard at the grammar school would become an important factor in his later business success. The curriculum was simple but thorough. Students learned penmanship, spelling, ciphering, and expressive reading. Particular care was taken to train students in pronunciation and graceful elocution. As well, students were instructed in languages, algebra, and geometry. Geography was taught with the use of globes, and students learned to construct maps. Astronomy, natural philosophy, and classics rounded out the curriculum.

In 1799 Samuel, then twelve years of age, was one of six children living in the Cunard cottage, which Abraham had expanded as the family had grown in size. During these years Abraham was one of three foreman–carpenters earning six shillings per diem in the Halifax Dockyard. They oversaw twenty-three carpenters who were paid a daily rate of five shillings. In 1799 Prince Edward, Duke of Kent and father to the future Queen Victoria, appointed Abraham master carpenter in the contingent branch of the engineering department. Now earning nine shillings per day, Abraham's future was secure. He would continue to work for the imperial government until his retirement in 1822.

According to the terms of his employment, Abraham was not at liberty to carry out any other type of business; presumably this provision was at some point revoked, because he also built houses privately. In this way he came to meet and gain the respect of many of the political and military elite in Halifax. His reputation as an exemplary carpenter was enhanced and soon spread throughout the community. He built a house for Nova Scotia Lieutenant-Governor John Coape Sherbrooke, spawning a relationship that would later benefit Samuel and him in their business pursuits.

As a boy, Samuel was rather unremarkable in appearance, but what he lacked physically he more than made up for in energy and initiative. From his early childhood he was never known to waste a single moment of the day. He was born with ambition and an unbending will to succeed, regardless of the task. Before he had become a teenager, Samuel had already developed business skills beyond his years, through his enterprise to sell remnants of lots on the waterfront. His boyhood experience of the buying, selling, and marketing of commodities—however small—gave him the confidence that would be the hallmark of his success in the years to come.

Samuel also became involved in community affairs early on. One of his first such activities occurred in 1809 when, at the age of twenty-two, he became a member of the exclusive Sun Fire Company, one of a number of volunteer fire companies in Halifax. Most buildings in Halifax at this time were made of wood, and the risk of fire was great. An out-of-control fire could quickly threaten the entire commercial centre of the town, and helping to prevent such fires was just plain good business.

Halifax was divided into fire wards, with a warden and committee responsible for fire control in each. The various fire companies were known as much for their social activities—like grand balls and sleigh rides—as for fighting fires, and with membership came a certain level of recognition and social standing. Samuel doubtless profited from his association with this fraternity. In 1821 he became president of the Sun Fire Company, and the Halifax Quarter Sessions appointed him a fire warden for the North Suburbs. For the next fourteen years he directed those fighting the flames and made decisions to demolish certain building in order to stop the spread of fire.

In 1830 his fellow fire wardens appointed him to a committee to have wells sunk on the lower side of Grand Parade, near the north barracks and the town clock. Also, the committee was to petition the lieutenant governor to construct two or three reservoirs on the eastern side of Citadel Hill. Samuel's experience with the Sun Fire Company would be reflected later in the great emphasis the Cunard Line placed on safety aboard its ships.

It was undoubtedly because of his father's influence, and perhaps also because of his involvement in the fire company, that in 1811

Samuel secured the position of the first clerk at the Engineer's Lumberyard, located at Greenbank, on the harbourfront in the South End of Halifax. For the next two years, under the direction of Captain Gustavus Nicolls of the Royal Engineers, Samuel gained valuable experience as a draftsman. He was paid seven shillings and six pence per diem, and twenty pounds per annum for lodging and office rent, one shilling daily for room, fuel, and candles, as well as a further daily shilling for rations. The experience he gained working under the tutelage of the senior draftsman, John George Toler, proved to be invaluable to both father and son when Abraham and Samuel went into business together under the firm name of A. Cunard and Son in or about 1812.

The firm was anchored by timber and the lucrative West Indian trade. At that time timber was a commodity highly sought after by the British Admiralty, which needed materials like spars and masts for its expanding fleet, and by the nearby Royal Navy Dockyard, for shipbuilding and repair. The time was opportune for Abraham and his younger partner. With considerable foresight, Abraham had secured in 1799 a grant of 1,000 acres of woodland in Cumberland County near the Pugwash River. In 1810 he had purchased nine parcels of timberland, totalling some 2,800 acres in nearby Tatamagouche. It was the beginning of the family's real estate holdings, which Samuel would greatly increase in the future.

The fledgling company enjoyed success and prosperity from its inception. As soon as the United States declared war in June 1812, Lieutenant-Governor Sir John Coape Sherbrooke began issuing licences to Halifax merchants to import American cargoes of provisions and naval stores as a means of getting around the American government's embargo on their export. Samuel Cunard—just twenty-five—received his licence in August; this underlines his standing and success as a young merchant. As well as American imports, A. Cunard and Son traded with the West Indies. Cunard's wharf was soon the place to find goods of all types, including spirits, molasses, brown sugar, and coffee from the islands of Martinique, Jamaica, and

Trinidad. At a prize auction in 1813, the Cunards purchased the company's first full-rigged ship, the *White Oak*, which was put immediately onto the London trade.

Two years later, Samuel Cunard married Susan Duffus, the sister of James, a man Samuel had befriended while attending the Halifax Grammar School. James was the son of William Duffus, who was born in Banff, Scotland, in 1762. William was a tailor who served his apprenticeship in Scotland before moving to London, where he worked in a tailor's shop for some time. In 1784, the year after Samuel's father and mother arrived in Nova Scotia, Duffus arranged passage to Halifax aboard the flagship of Admiral Sir Charles Douglas. He set up his business and in 1786 married Mary McNeill. His business prospered; with Britain at war, uniforms were in great demand. After giving birth to five children, all but James dying in infancy, Mary passed away in 1792.

After a brief courtship, William married Susannah Murdoch in 1794. She was the attractive daughter of the Reverend James Murdoch, who lived in the Annapolis Valley village of Horton. They soon became known in Halifax as the most handsome couple in town. William, with his tall, noble, and commanding presence, would often be seen horseback riding with Susannah, or Susan, as she was often called. The latter frequently appeared in her scarlet habit topped with a beaver hat and feather. Their union produced six more Duffus children, the first of whom was Susan Duffus, born May 25, 1795. While it was said that none of the offspring could compare in looks with their parents, Susan caught the eye of Samuel Cunard. They were married by the Reverend Robert Stanser at St. Paul's Church on February 4, 1815.

Like his father before him, Samuel arranged to construct a new home for his wife and family-to-be. It was a modest but substantial four-storey dwelling on the east side of Brunswick Street, fast becoming a fashionable area of Halifax; the cottage where Samuel and his eight brothers and sisters had been born was just to the rear, where it retained a commanding view of Halifax Harbour.

By 1815 Samuel had become quite accustomed to conducting business in a wartime economy, and had already assumed the leading role in A. Cunard and Son. Born with a strong work ethic, he was customarily at the wharves before dawn each day, buying cargoes from the West Indies and also those brought in under government licence from the United States until peace came in 1815. A. Cunard and Son was founded and prospered upon Samuel's energy, reliability, and good reputation, aided perhaps by Abraham's widespread acquaintance with the business and political elite of Halifax gained while master carpenter in the engineering department.

After the war, the Cunards further consolidated their land holdings in the North Suburbs of Halifax by acquiring land now surplus to the military but very valuable to the company for wharves and warehouses. Their reputation as respectable Halifax merchants is evidenced from the support for their petition for land by surveyor Charles Morris, who noted "their well known character, for active exertion and enterprise in useful improvements and commercial pursuits."

The foundation had been laid for a company that would capture the imagination of the world.

CHAPTER 3

GROWTH OF A BUSINESS

AND THE BEGINNINGS

OF STEAM

The company of A. Cunard and Son continued to meet with success. One early contract negotiated by the company was the successful tender in 1815 to supply a hundred-ton vessel for government service. Its intended use was to protect trade and fisheries, prevent smuggling, sail to New York for mail in winter, transport the lieutenant-governor on official tours, and move men or supplies to military outposts. The tender was won by the firm with its purchase of a sloop, the *Earl Bathurst*, for the sum of 1,500 pounds. (This vessel was soon deemed to be too small and was replaced in 1817 with a larger ship, the brig *Chebucto*, on which Samuel's brother Edward would serve as master.)

Communication in the nineteenth century was, of course, considerably slower than it is today. In Cunard's day, commerce was totally dependent on the passage of mail between Britain and its colonies across the storm-tossed Atlantic in British North America. The written word, committed to paper by quill pen, was, until the emergence of the telegraph and telephone, the only way to communicate and transact business. The news from the continent, and the colonists' only means of learning what was happening in the rest of the world, was delivered by means of the unscheduled and erratic arrival of the newspapers from Britain by ship. The "news" was often weeks or months old by the time it reached its intended readers. Despite the uncertainty and tardiness of delivery, the arrival of the English mails was always an event looked forward to with great anticipation in the colonies.

During the War of 1812, Falmouth packets, or "coffin brigs," as they were called, had delivered all the overseas mail bound for the British colonies to Bermuda, where letter bags consigned to Halifax had been picked up by the first ship going in that direction—often a Cunard vessel heading back home from the West Indies. In this manner, Samuel Cunard became familiar with the carriage of mails, as it then was, and built a reputation for steady, reliable service with the Home Office back in England.

When peace returned, the Falmouth packets resumed their prewar schedule, which had them call at Halifax and New York in summer and deliver mail to Bermuda only during winter months. When Bermuda protested, the British government relented and agreed to inaugurate a mail service between Halifax and the islands, including Bermuda and Newfoundland. Cunard was for the first time engaged in the timely, scheduled delivery of the mails. He provided two small brigs, *Susan* and *Emily*, under contract to the British Admiralty to carry the mail from Bermuda to Halifax. He had used *Chebucto* on a winter mail run between Halifax and New York, which gave him insight into procedures for handling of the mails, and the Bermuda–Halifax run was his first official mail contract.

Cunard could and did deliver, but the scheduling and arrival of his ships was entirely dependent upon the arrival of the Falmouth packets from England, whose schedules were in turn subject to wind and weather. Sometimes the Atlantic crossing would take as many as twelve weeks; it was impossible to predict when the mail would arrive from the England. Cunard was already thinking of how the situation could be improved.

If timely arrival of the mails via the government packets was unreliable, the distribution of the English mails from Halifax to the various outports of the colonies was even more uncertain. The St. Lawrence River was frozen in the winter months, prohibiting delivery of the mails by ship to Quebec City. Cunard recognized this and quickly established a system whereby the mails were carried on horseback by riders from Halifax to Annapolis Royal (140 miles away on the Bay of Fundy), across to Saint John by ship, and up the St. John River by canoe to the beginning of an overland trail. From there the mail was carried by foot more than 200 miles through swamps and forests to the St. Lawrence and on to Quebec City. This was known as Cunard's Overland Express.

During the summer months, once the mails had been landed at Halifax, Cunard would send them on his ships to Quebec City via the St. Lawrence River, departing from the port of Pictou, located in northern Nova Scotia on the Northumberland Strait. First, however, the mail had to be moved from Halifax to Pictou, and to do this Cunard created another overland trail, eventually to become a stagecoach run through the woods, north from Halifax to Truro, then north and east from Truro over Mount Thom and on to Pictou, a distance of about a hundred miles.

The service was such a success that in 1816, when the mails contract was to be renewed, the British post office added delivery of mails to Boston as well as Bermuda. In winter the mail for Quebec went to Boston and overland from there, bypassing Halifax. These early mail contracts considerably enhanced Cunard's rapport with government officials, added greatly to the company fortunes, and represented the beginning of Cunard's long career in the postal system.

Over the course of the next few years, Samuel and Abraham continued to expand the company's fleet of sailing vessels. Between 1815 and 1818, Samuel Cunard became the registered owner of six vessels, including three schooners, two sloops, and one brig, ranging in size from 42 to 133 tons, all purchased at auction. In these early days of the Cunard enterprise it was common to purchase a vessel for a modest sum, and when opportunity presented itself, to sell at a profit, using the income to expand the size of the fleet. With increased prosperity the company would later contract for the construction of its own ships.

Also in 1815 came perhaps the first manifestation of Samuel's interest in steam power, a phenomenon that was slowly but steadily growing around the world. The concept of steam navigation was already centuries old. The Spanish, French, and English had experimented with steam as early as the sixteenth century, and in 1769 Englishman James Watt produced a successful steam engine. John Fitch, an engineer who hailed from Windsor, Connecticut, experimented in the late 1700s with different means of applying steam to boat propulsion, including mechanical oar, paddlewheel, and screw. During this time he operated a regular steam passage service on the Delaware River and, like Cunard, knew that steam would "be the method of crossing the Atlantic, whether I bring it to perfection or not."

Robert Fulton, born on a small farm at Little Britain (now Fulton) in Pennsylvania, capitalized upon and made practical use of the dreams and aspirations of his predecessors. The result was the *Clermont*, America's first commercially successful steamship, launched from the Charles Brown shipyard on the East River in 1807. On September 11, 1807, this paddlewheeler successfully navigated the Hudson River from New York upriver to Albany and back, averaging five knots under steam. One of the passengers aboard the maiden voyage is reputed to have been Samuel Cunard.

In 1809 Canada's first successful steamer appeared on the St. Lawrence River. John Molson, the beer baron in Montreal, saw the opportunity afforded by steam to expedite the movement of his product on the great inland waterway that was the St. Lawrence River. He financed the construction of the steamship *Accommodation*, which that year made the passage from Montreal to Quebec City and thereafter became a regular sight plying the St. Lawrence.

Inspired by these successes, Samuel, together with a group of prominent Halifax businessmen, was instrumental in forming the Halifax Steamboat Company, which was dedicated to improving the ferry service between Halifax and Dartmouth, on the opposite side of the harbour. Ferries had been operating there since 1752, under sail, oar, and eventually horse power, and the crossing time was often thirty minutes, depending on weather conditions. Sometimes the elements would conspire against the little ferry transports, and it was not uncommon for passengers to find themselves fetched up on McNab's Island, out towards the harbour mouth. As both Halifax and Dartmouth were settled and commerce grew, it was inevitable that the ferry link would take on increased interest to those who stood to profit most from improvements in service.

Even though steam was a relatively new phenomenon, and had not yet appeared locally, Cunard and the other founders of the Halifax Steamboat Company, with considerable personal knowledge of Maritime trading and local commerce, set about to improve the ferry service. They focused their attention on how best the steam engine might be utilized to attain this goal. Soon after the steamboat company was formed, contact was made with manufacturers and owners in New York, where construction and employment of steam ferries had proliferated since Watt's success with the *Clermont* on the Hudson River. Although it would still be some years before a steam ferry would connect Halifax to Dartmouth (for a number of years, while the directors grappled with the concept and costs of steam vessels, the company continued to use horses and operated as the "Halifax Team-Boat Company"), Samuel Cunard would remain an interested observer and participant in the movement to mechanize the ferry service.

Proving early his aptitude for handling many different ventures at once, Cunard was also at this time making his first attempt to revive the whaling industry in Nova Scotia. For a number of years during the latter part of the eighteenth century, a group of Quaker loyalists from Nantucket had operated a fleet of whalers out of Dartmouth, Nova Scotia. It was a substantial industry, employing twenty-seven ships in the South Atlantic, the crews and supplies required to outfit voyages, as well as the onshore support facilities, like cooperages and blacksmith shops, required to service the fleet. Samuel was told much of this by his father, for in 1792, when Samuel was only five years old, the British government directed that the entire whaling fleet be relocated to Milford Haven, from which port they would henceforth operate in an attempt to bolster Britain's whaling industry. Overnight the ships, whalers, and their families were gone to Wales, and across the Narrows from the Cunard home their houses stood empty and their wharves idle.

Samuel retained this memory, and aspired to build up a whaling fleet to replace the one taken from his community years before. In 1817 A. Cunard and Son outfitted the brig *Rachel* on a summer whaling cruise to the Strait of Belle Isle. This and other expeditions that followed proved to be failures. The Cunards persisted, however, and were successful in obtaining government subsidies to underwrite the substantial costs associated with a whaling trip to the South Atlantic whaling grounds. Their rationale and ultimate success in securing bounties was due to their ability to convince the government that if the industry were revived, the whole country would benefit. In 1819 the brig *Prince of Waterloo* was outfitted and dispatched to the South Atlantic, returning home almost two years later with hardly enough cargo to pay for the cost of the voyage. With these failures, Cunard chose to focus his attention on other enterprises. He would return to whaling again in 1827.

These early forays into the whaling grounds, although unprofitable, did reveal a bold and enterprising entrepreneurial spirit in the person of Samuel Cunard. They also created a rapport between Samuel, the young businessman, and government circles in Halifax.

Cunard was also busy at this time proving his value as a citizen of Halifax and of the British Empire. Trusted by his peers and those in power, he was engaged in many different pursuits, the aforementioned Sun Fire Company being just one. In 1816, at the age of twenty-nine, he had become a commissioner of the lighthouses on the coasts of Nova Scotia, a position he held for the next twenty years, overseeing the construction of about one new lighthouse per year.

He was also chosen to help alleviate the plight of Halifax's many poor after the war. Halifax was, in peacetime, experiencing a major depression in trade. The arrival of large numbers of immigrants further worsened the situation. Local work was scarce and without it the new arrivals could provide neither food nor shelter for themselves. In an attempt to deal with the influx, Lieutenant-Governor Dalhousie in 1817 selected two Halifax businessmen, Samuel Cunard and Michael Tobin, to assist penniless immigrants from Newfoundland and Europe. Funding was provided for food and transportation to move the newcomers to other parts of the province, where room and board could be secured in return for work throughout the winter. For those facing starvation in Halifax, Cunard and Tobin, aided by Susan Cunard and Tobin's wife, opened a soup kitchen where hundreds were served daily. This humanitarian aid would become a regular feature of life in Halifax for many years.

As the second decade of the nineteenth century came to a close, Samuel decided to diversify his business in a way which would have a tremendous impact on its immediate fortunes. In 1819 the firm received a new, expanded contract — arising out of the earlier contract to deliver mails in Boston and Bermuda — to carry the mail by sailing packet between Halifax and Boston, Newfoundland, and Bermuda. From this moment on, the company fortunes would escalate at a rapid pace, led by the untiring energy and initiative of Samuel Cunard. Only six years from its inception, A. Cunard and Son was already a company in transition. Change was afoot and would accelerate rapidly following the retirement of Abraham from the business in 1820.

CHAPTER 4

EXPANSION AND
NEW VENTURES

Margaret Cunard, Samuel's mother, had been in failing health for many years. The physical demands brought on by giving birth to nine children had taken a toll, and neither Abraham nor Margaret had ever fully gotten over the death of their first child, Mary. She had married John Parr, a master mariner from Liverpool who worked in His Majesty's Transport Service. John, Mary, and an infant daughter, Margaret Ann, were all killed by yellow fever in Bridgetown, Barbados, in January 1811. This tragedy aged both parents, leaving Samuel, the next eldest, to play a prominent role in the upbringing and education of all his younger brothers and sisters, despite his preoccupation with his business and his new bride.

There was a considerable age difference between Samuel, twenty-eight in 1814, and his younger brothers, Henry, John and Thomas, aged eleven, thirteen, and fifteen respectively, and Samuel certainly adopted a fatherly approach in arranging their educations. He sent them to Pictou Academy, some hundred miles northwest of Halifax, established by Reverend Thomas McCulloch, a Scot, a few years earlier. In a letter to McCulloch dated September 7, 1815, Samuel makes his views on the subject of education very clear. Referring to the fifteen-year-old John, who had just returned from a year at sea, Samuel writes:

> I have again taken the liberty to send you another pupil to whom I must beg your attention. The Masters under whose care he has been heretofore have paid but little attention to his improvement and what he has learned at school he has forgotten within the last year at sea. He will require to commence at the first rudiments. I wish him taught what I requested you to teach the other boys [Thomas and Henry] — and I hope within one year (the time I propose leaving him with you) that he will have made considerable improvement, particularly as he is now of an age to perceive the want of education.

The other two brothers, Thomas and Henry, had already been pupils at Pictou Academy; Samuel used typically plain language to suggest to the headmaster what he thought best for their continuing education:

> If you think it best, I have no objection to Henry and Thomas learning Latin. I think I stated to you in my last, the only reason I have for not requesting you to teach them Latin — namely that they are intended for business and that a plain English education answers the purpose. You will say that I have very contracted views — and I must allow it.

Just as he took charge of his brothers' educations, Samuel also took charge of his parents' comfort. In 1815–16 he purchased a large property of five hundred acres from the heirs of John McGuire in Rawdon, near to property owned and occupied by members of

Margaret Cunard's immediate family. He then arranged for the construction of a retirement home for his parents upon the property. It was a comfortable one-and-a-half-storey house anchored by a massive central fireplace, butler's pantry, barn, and several out-buildings.

By this time, Samuel was the principal of A. Cunard and Son — with his passion for business, he had long since assumed the dominant role in the company. Still two years away from retirement from the dockyard, Abraham was ready to retire from the family business and move to the Rawdon house. In doing so, he relieved Samuel from the burden of caring for his mother, whose health was deteriorating. Following Abraham's withdrawal from the business in 1820, he, sixty-four, and Margaret, sixty-two, moved into their new home in Rawdon. Their retirement, however, was all too brief. Margaret had only one year to enjoy her new home and the company of her nearby family; she died in December 1821, at the age of sixty-three. Abraham carried on for a few years after his wife's death, retiring from the dockyard in 1822, and then passed away in January 1824, at the age of sixty-eight. While his health had been failing, his death was perhaps hurried on with the news just a few weeks before of his son William's drowning. William had been a passenger aboard the ship *Wyton*, lost at sea off Cape North, Cape Breton Island, on November 23, 1823. When the news finally reached Halifax, William's death was much lamented. Both parents were buried in the cemetery of St. Paul's Anglican Church in Centre Rawdon. William's body was not recovered.

With both parents now gone, Samuel's brothers John, Thomas, and Edward pursued careers at sea as masters aboard various vessels in the Cunard fleet of sailing ships. Henry, who had gone to help out with his parents' last few years in Rawdon, moved to Chatham, New Brunswick, to work with brother Joseph, whom Samuel had set up in a timber and shipbuilding business under the name of Joseph Cunard and Company in 1820. The firm was established across the river from Newcastle. Joseph, twelve years younger than Samuel and his opposite in almost every way, was flamboyant, boisterous, and lacking in the business ability of his older brother. Samuel probably hoped that Henry, mild-mannered and much more like Samuel, would be a subduing influence on their outrageous brother. In the end, this would not be the case, but Samuel's worries about Joseph were probably assuaged for a time in the 1820s.

Samuel dissolved the old firm of A. Cunard and Son in the spring of 1824, "the business heretofore conducted by that firm to be carried on under the firm of Samuel Cunard and Company," and later shortened the new name to S. Cunard and Company. Abraham had left a will in which he named his three eldest sons, Samuel, Joseph, and William, as trustees. As William had perished, Samuel and Joseph wound up the estate in 1826 by dividing the Halifax properties amongst themselves and brother Edward, who had been taken into the family business in 1825. The younger brothers, John, Thomas, and Henry, did not share in the estate. Samuel's two sisters, Mary and Susan, pre-deceased their father.

With full control of the Halifax waterfront commercial property, Samuel Cunard was in a position to move forward with plans to expand his business interests. Samuel continued to be incredibly involved with his community during these years; for example, in 1822 he and eight other merchants in Halifax formed a committee of trade that would recommend on the propriety of forming a chamber of commerce. Out of this initiative came the Nova Scotia Commercial Society, which annually elected fifteen members by ballot to form an executive, known as a chamber of commerce, which in turn would elect a president and other officers.

Throughout the remaining years of the 1820s, under Samuel's ownership, S. Cunard and Company greatly expanded its fleet. By the end of the decade there were more than forty-five sailing vessels registered to Samuel Cunard. For the most part they were previously owned vessels, built in New Brunswick, Nova Scotia, Prince Edward Island, and England for the coastal trade. They were sloops, schooners, and brigs averaging 50 to 250 tons burthen. A few notable exceptions included the full-rigged ship *Samuel Cunard*, 303 tons, built by Samuel's brother-in-law William Duffus in Big Bras d'Or, Cape Breton Island, in 1827, and the ship *Rose*, 416 tons, built in Brighthelmsea, England, in 1826.

With the expansion of the fleet came increased opportunities to bolster the West India trade. The Cunard wharves located off Upper Water Street became the busiest of the many commercial wharves that sprouted out from the Halifax waterfront. Cunard ships soon became familiar sights on the sea lanes between Halifax, South America, and Newfoundland. Cunard packets delivered passengers and mail to Boston and Bermuda. The Cunard wharves were piled high with trade goods for shipment outbound—fish and timber for the West Indies—and inbound cargoes of sugar, rum, molasses, and coffee from the Caribbean and South America.

The land adjacent to the Cunard wharves, which had been purchased with considerable foresight years earlier, now proved its worth. In 1824 Samuel built a large four-storey warehouse, using ironstone from the quarries at nearby Purcell's Cove. A magnificent freestone arch mortised into the centre of the 110-foot-long structure gave access directly off Upper Water Street to the Cunard wharves, which fast became the centre of Cunard's commercial empire. They were located just down the hill and only a short walk from the Cunard home on Brunswick Street.

Cunard continuously sought ways to improve and expand his mercantile interests. Such an opportunity presented itself in the lucrative tea business. The East India Company was a venerable firm that in the mid-1820s still controlled trade with China; at this time the British colonies were prohibited from having any direct trade with that country. Tea was a highly sought-after commodity both in Britain and the colonies. Historically, London was the distribution centre for China teas, but in 1824 Cunard learned of a proposal to ship tea directly from Canton to Quebec in East India Company ships. Cunard immediately boarded a ship bound for London, where he arranged to meet with East India Company officials. Samuel was comfortable at sea and used the seven-week crossing under sail to formulate his plan for securing the tea contract. Upon arrival, in presenting his case to the world's tea barons, Samuel displayed his practical business approach.

Originally, S. Cunard and Company made a joint application with the firm of Venner, Brown, and Wheeler, of Saint John, for "the importation of tea into the ports of Halifax, NS, and St. John, N.B." In a personal interview with William Astell, chairman of the East India Company, both companies stressed their "residence in the provinces, a thorough knowledge of the trade and people, and the possession of every convenience in fireproof warehouses." Their submission was accompanied by a letter from Bainbridge and Brown, London commission merchants and ship brokers, offering security for the applicants. They noted, "These gentlemen are the partners in two of the oldest establishments in Halifax and St. John, possessing people, capital, excellent warehouses of their own and thoroughly acquainted with the business and people of their respective provinces."

Ultimately, it was Samuel Cunard alone who secured the agency. He convinced the East India Company directors that coastal trade was increasing daily, and that tea could "be conveyed by water in two days from Halifax to any part on [sic] New Brunswick, at very moderate expense." It was Cunard's direct, no-nonsense, practical approach in his London meetings, as well as the support of London's influential John Bainbridge, that won Cunard the contract. With his considerable background and familiarity with shipping in and around the Maritime Provinces and Quebec, Cunard convinced company officials that contrary winds and winter ice conditions in the St. Lawrence River made it impossible for the Maritime Provinces to receive their annual tea supply from Quebec. After five months in London negotiating with East India Company officials, Cunard successfully secured the agency for the delivery of tea directly to Nova Scotia. By the time he returned to Halifax he had been away for seven months during which time Susan had given birth to a son, William. It was quite a homecoming—a new son and the prized tea agency, which Cunard retained for the next thirty-seven years. Although his commission was only two percent, the tea trade provided him with a steady flow of capital and broadened his business interests.

Cunard took considerable satisfaction from having wrested the lucrative East India tea agency from the grasp of another prominent Halifax businessman, Enos Collins. Collins had made a fortune from privateering, and was reputed to be the richest man in Nova Scotia. It was not uncommon for him to use his immense wealth to sway public officials from time to time, including Lieutenant-Governor James Kempt, whom he periodically threatened with moving to the United States with his fortune. While Collins and Kempt cooled their heels in Halifax, Samuel was successfully negotiating with the East India Company in London.

The first of the China tea clippers, the *Countess of Harcourt*, entered Halifax Harbour on May 29, 1826. A crowd on Long Wharf cheered the vessel as it passed up the harbour. It then tied up at the Cunard wharf, where it proceeded to unload 6,517 chests and boxes of tea with such names as Bohea, Congo, Souchong, and Hyson, which the East India Company shipped directly from China. The arrival of the "East Indiaman"—the name given to ships of the East India Company—was hailed by all, particularly the older women in town, as "the advent of a new era in the history of tea drinkers. Shrub, peppermint, clove water and aniseed were to be considered among the discarded beverages from that day. The tea was to be had in an unadulterated state, and cheap withal."

From this time the Cunard wharves became a great object of attraction, first because the *Countess of Harcourt* came from such an immense distance, and second because its cargo was all tea. The ship smelled like a teapot! It was a large vessel, too, perhaps 1,200 tons, a monster at that time for a merchant. Haligonians had previously thought trade consisted of brigs running to the West Indies, but this

China tea clipper hailed from the East, "just where about the sun gets up in the morning to make his run for the day."

The precious cargo was stored in the commodious Cunard warehouse. As agent for the East India Company, Cunard advertised that a public sale would be held on June 19, 1826, with all the tea open to inspection for five days before, and on the sale date a printed catalogue would be available. In ensuing years, local Halifax newspapers would regularly advertise quarterly auctions of China teas from Cunard's wharf. Before each sale the company published a catalogue, and just before an auction began, prospective purchasers had the opportunity to view the different teas for sale. Cunard was frequently the auctioneer, and it was not uncommon for hundreds of chests of tea to be bid upon at quarterly sales.

The months spent in London procuring the tea agency proved valuable to Cunard in many other ways. During this time he was able to familiarize himself with the city of London and establish contact with London merchants and officials in the British Office of Trade and Plantations, responsible for colonial policy and administration. Typical of the many contacts who would help play a role in expanding his business empire was John Bainbridge, the commission merchant and ship broker with the London firm Bainbridge and Brown, which provided bonds as security in support of Cunard's bid for the tea agency. Bainbridge was also an active member of a committee of London merchants trading in British North America. This group had a particular interest in the timber trade, which Cunard was busily expanding, through his brother Joseph, in New Brunswick at this time. While Cunard was in London, Bainbridge was appointed provincial agent for the Nova Scotia legislature in London. Samuel would often express his gratitude for new relationships by naming company ships after his friends. The *John Bainbridge* was one such vessel.

Travelling about London, meeting and mixing with government officials and members of the British mercantile class, gave Cunard a tremendous advantage over his peers in Halifax who chose to run their businesses from the comfort of their offices in that distant port. The ability to listen, observe and present himself to the London establishment was an advantage that he would exploit to the fullest and would ultimately set Cunard apart from contemporaries back home who conducted their business through the impersonal and irregular postal system.

Cunard was a bold businessman, ever eager to join in new initiatives and enterprises, and given the wide scope of his business interests and the generation of wealth that flowed from those pursuits, it is not surprising that Cunard would eventually become involved in the financial sector. Until 1825 the monetary system in the colonies was confused. As much as England wanted the colonies to use British money, the colonists made frequent use of American dollars and Spanish silver, not to mention metal tokens of different types issued by local merchants. It was commonplace but awkward — and potentially dangerous, especially for those engaged in business — to carry silver or coinage physically upon one's person.

In 1825 Samuel Cunard and various other established moneylenders in the city, including Enos Collins, joined together in forming the colony's first bank. Cunard became an original partner in the Halifax Banking Company, which would later evolve into the Canadian Imperial Bank of Commerce. As with all his business pursuits, Cunard's participation was not token in nature. He subscribed five thousand of fifty thousand pounds of capital for the fledgling Halifax Banking Company, also known as Cogswell's Bank, named after Henry Cogswell, the first president of the institution.

The profits made by the shareholders were enormous, but were condoned on the grounds that they put a good deal of money into circulation, which offered "great convenience to those in trade." Not surprisingly, in time, there was a groundswell of dissatisfaction with the concentration of so much wealth in the hands of so few. In response, another of Canada's chartered banks, the Bank of Nova Scotia, was formed in 1832 as a rival of the Halifax Banking

Company. Eventually, in 1836, Cunard withdrew from the Halifax Banking Company and became a resident director of the London-based Bank of British North America.

Another venture in which Cunard was an active participant was the Shubenacadie Canal. From firsthand experience on his own vessels, Cunard was well aware of the danger inherent in the long sea voyage around the coast of Nova Scotia to the Bay of Fundy. He had long dreamed of the day when ships travelling between Halifax and Saint John, New Brunswick, could avoid this long and perilous passage. Cunard purchased forty shares and became one of the first backers of the Shubenacadie Canal Company. It was incorporated in 1826 to create a system of lakes and canals from Dartmouth, across the harbour from Halifax, to Minas Basin on the Bay of Fundy. Cunard later became vice-president of the company.

The undertaking to build a system of canals and waterways across the province was the largest engineering project to that time in Nova Scotia, and the work of building the canal went on for many years. As construction continued, the company ran into serious financial difficulties. In 1853, a new company, Inland Navigation Company, took over the task of completing the canal. Cunard, in his remarkably unwavering support for the project, purchased twenty-five shares of the fifteen hundred allocated under incorporation. Although the Shubenacadie Canal went into operation in 1861, it could not compete with the railways and in a few years ceased operations. While it proved to be one of those few business ventures in which Cunard did not succeed, the Shubenacadie Canal initiative, and his support for it, was important if for no other reason than it galvanized local interest in a major engineering project, similar in size and scope to others in Upper Canada.

In 1827, Cunard made his final attempt to revive the whaling industry he had first tried to revitalize a decade earlier. He became a trustee and shareholder, along with his brothers Joseph and Edward, in the Halifax Whaling Company, a joint stock company that enjoyed the financial support of a number of others in the city's mercantile sector. In anticipation of this venture, S. Cunard and Company had built and launched the whaling ship *Pacific*, which set off for the South Pacific early that year.

Ultimately the whaling industry ceased altogether. The costs far exceeded the returns from voyages to the far-flung whaling grounds. The poor results could not, however, be categorized as absolute failure. Again, largely through Cunard initiative, local interests had been inspired to action — contracts let, supplies purchased, ships built, jobs created and hopes and aspirations born. As was so often the case in Halifax during the growth of S. Cunard and Company, the firm created work and employment, particularly in shipbuilding in tough times, post-war depressions and the boom-and-bust cycle that has historically been part of growth in the Maritimes. And shipbuilding contracts were not restricted to the Halifax area. Cunard was often in the forefront of creating employment throughout the Maritime Provinces — sometimes creating employment and industry where before there were none. One case in point was the construction of the *Samuel Cunard*, built by Samuel's brother-in-law, William Duffus, at Big Bras d'Or Cape Breton in 1827. It, along with the 421-ton *Rose*, toiled unsuccessfully in the South Pacific for many years, until Samuel shut down the venture completely.

Never one to be overcome by failures, Samuel dove headlong into yet another project in 1827. Another agency was in the offing — one that would give Samuel Cunard access to Nova Scotia's rich coal resources, and would be pivotal in the history of transatlantic navigation. Black gold, as the French called it, was first discovered in outcrop seams on the shores of Cape Breton Island in 1672 by the French explorer Nicolas Denys. The actual mining of coal took place at Cow Bay in 1720, and the coal was supplied to the fortress at Louisbourg and exported to Boston. Coal was also discovered in Pictou County in 1809, and was for well over a century the mainstay of industry there.

In September 1817, Lieutenant-Governor Lord Dalhousie paid a visit to the coalfields of the East River, near Pictou. Dalhousie had recently received orders from England to lease these fields on behalf of the Crown. Admiral David Milne accompanied him; Milne had some knowledge of mineralogy and coal mining in England and Lord Dalhousie was anxious to secure his opinion as to the quality and quantity of coal on this site. It was Sir David's opinion that the coal was of excellent quality and, with easy access for water transport, showed great development potential.

That same year Lord Dalhousie had his first experience aboard a vessel propelled by steam and fueled by coal. He had traveled by steamboat from Saint John up the St. John River to Fredericton, New Brunswick. There were also a number of small "steamboats" operating on the St. Lawrence River between Quebec and Montreal at this time.

Samuel Cunard was very aware of this. Even as the first coal was being extracted from Nova Scotia soil, the man who was now owner of the largest fleet of sailing ships on this side of the Atlantic was firming up in his own mind that the way of the future lay in steam — and the fact that coal could provide the fuel for the steam engine was not lost on Samuel.

Cunard's first attempt to acquire control of Nova Scotia's coal mines occurred in 1826. He made a proposal to Sir James Kempt, now lieutenant-governor of Nova Scotia, to lease the coal mines of Cape Breton. He proposed a thirty-year term with a royalty of two shillings per chaldron (or thirty-six bushels) on all coal shipments over sixty thousand chaldrons. Cunard's initiative however, was delayed by one of history's foibles.

A few years earlier, King George III had been suffering some embarrassment at the hands of his son, the Duke of York. The latter was a compulsive gambler and had incurred huge gambling debts. In an effort to help him out of his financial difficulties, the king gave his son a sixty-year lease of all mines and minerals in distant Nova Scotia. Following his father's death in 1820, the Duke of York was faced with financial ruin. His entire income was consumed by simply paying the interest on his accumulated debts. One of his primary creditors was the firm of Rundle, Bridge and Rundle, court jewellers whose later claim to fame was the creation of the crown used in the coronation of Queen Victoria and all succeeding English monarchs.

The jewellery firm owned a company called the General Mining Association, which had been engaged in an unsuccessful exploration for minerals in South America. When it learned that the Duke now possessed all the mineral rights to Nova Scotia, a deal was negotiated to relieve him of his debts and to pay him a small percentage of profits in exchange for the mining rights. Coal was the primary resource available in the province. Shortly after the deal was consummated in 1826, the GMA, as it came to be known, sent a mining engineer named George Blackwell to Halifax to investigate and report on the potential for opening mines in Nova Scotia. While in Halifax, Blackwell had several meetings with Cunard, who, to help get the GMA started, offered the use of his ships as well as wharves and waterfront property in Halifax. Samuel was competing with the well-established local firm of Belcher, Binney and Company for the cherished position as agent for the GMA, and his offer was accepted in 1827.

Cunard and the GMA moved rapidly to open mines and refine the process for the mining of coal in Nova Scotia. They began mining in Pictou County, one hundred miles north of Halifax. Soon the company expanded operations to the Sydney area on Cape Breton Island, north of Pictou and separated from mainland Nova Scotia by the waters of the Strait of Canso. The discovery of deep seams of coal led to the opening of mines by the GMA at Sydney Mines and Bridgeport. As agent for the GMA, Cunard oversaw much of the development of coalfields and the evolution of the coal industry in Nova Scotia. This had a profound effect upon his education in and preoccupation with steam.

So did the arrival of Nova Scotia's first stationary steam engine. On the recommendation of the British Government, the GMA appointed Richard Smith, an engineer, as operations manager in Nova Scotia. On June 4, 1827, Smith, together with scores of miners from England, arrived in the Pictou harbour aboard the Cunard ship *Margaret Pilkington*. The vessel was loaded with mining equipment of all kinds, including Nova Scotia's first stationary steam engine and pumping apparatus. It dropped anchor at the mouth of the East River and within a very short time began to offload its cargo. Onlookers from nearby Pictou were astonished when a huge iron boiler, part of the steam engine complement, was literally thrown overboard. Instead of sinking, as onlookers expected, the boiler floated and was towed up the East River to Stellarton. There, in the Albion Mine, the engine and pumping apparatus were installed and started up at the official opening ceremonies, held on December 7, 1827. The stationary steam engine facilitated the pumping of water and hoisting from the mine shafts that ran deep beneath the surface in this Pictou County coalfield.

Dignitaries from all over the province attended this historic event. Among them was Samuel Cunard, who perhaps reflected on the marvels of steam and the seemingly limitless supply of coal literally at his feet. Steam and coal — for Samuel Cunard, the present and the future were drawing ever closer together.

Despite his overwhelming preoccupation with the East India and General Mining Association agencies, Cunard remained very much involved with family. The post-war depression that had settled over Halifax following 1815 had a severe impact upon the Duffus family fortunes. The tailoring business so successfully established by William Duffus languished as demand for uniforms fell in peacetime conditions. Samuel arranged to put his in-laws back on good financial good footing with a comfortable living allowance. His mother-in-law, Susannah, who was very fond of her grandchildren, devoted more and more of her time in helping with care of the growing young Cunard family. Unbeknownst to her, she would soon assume a much greater role as a grandmother.

In February of 1827, Samuel's wife Susan had given birth to their eighth child, Isabella. Samuel had been spending more time of late with his eldest son Edward, affectionately known as Ned. Sam had taken Ned with him to the recent celebrations in Pictou County. They had made the trip up on one of the Cunard vessels, and had returned by stagecoach. Edward was a boy of twelve, but like his father before him, was quickly learning the ways of business.

The euphoria arising from the GMA event at the Albion Mine was followed by a large family gathering for Christmas at the Cunard home. It was the last Christmas that Samuel would share with his whole family. On January 23, 1828, Susan gave birth to their ninth child, Elizabeth. The newborn would survive, but the mother would not. Susan Cunard died ten days later, leaving Samuel in charge of both a large young family and a burgeoning commercial empire.

CHAPTER 5

FAMILY MATTERS AND A GRAND APPOINTMENT

V ery little has been recorded about the relatively short and understated life of Susan Cunard. She did, however, play a key role as a wife and mother in raising a young family and attending to many social and personal affairs while Samuel was busy building his commercial empire. By the time she was thirty-three, she had produced six daughters and two sons, all of whom received her constant care and attention while growing up in the Cunard household on Brunswick Street. In her thirteen years of married life Susan devoted all her time to her husband and family. But for this, Samuel Cunard might never have risen to prominence within the Halifax commercial elite, or, later, the broader international marketplace.

Samuel was devastated by the loss of his wife. Standing over her gravesite in the Old Burying Ground opposite St. Matthew's Church in Halifax, Samuel Cunard felt not only the loss of a wife, but also the weight of the responsibility he now had: to fill the void in his children's lives left by his wife's death.

Adding to this challenge was the age of his young family—Elizabeth was newborn, and the eldest was just thirteen. To this point, all had been raised in a warm and loving home anchored by their mother's care. Further complicating the picture was the increased responsibility Samuel had assumed in looking after his own younger siblings after the death of his parents just a few years earlier. Fortunately, five surviving brothers, although considerably younger than he, had by the time of Susan's death matured and had been placed by Samuel within various branches of the family business.

Also fortunately for Samuel, the close bond between the Cunard and Duffus families had only grown with time. Following her daughter's death, Susannah Duffus came to Samuel's aid and devoted herself entirely to helping him care for his bereaved young family. "Dear Grandmother Duffus," as the children always called her in later years, was the beloved matriarch of the clan. Warmhearted, untiring in her management of family affairs, always first on the scene in sickness or trouble, she still rode every morning on the Halifax Common, erect and graceful as a girl beside her tall husband. In addition to the direct intervention of Grandmother Duffus, the Cunard children continued to receive the attention and support of the extended Cunard family — aunts, uncles, and cousins who had always been, but were now more than ever, there when needed.

For the first time in his busy life, Samuel Cunard, ever driven by an unbridled sense of purpose and achievement, slowed down to take stock of his life, and to focus on that which he valued more than anything else — his family. For the next two years, between 1828 and 1830, Cunard stayed close to home while his family adapted to the loss of their mother. During this time Samuel devoted as much of his time as possible to his children. Despite the unrelenting demands made upon him with the increasing fortunes of S. Cunard and Company, Samuel refrained from taking business trips too far away from his family for extended periods of time until he felt comfortable with their home life and well-being. He would often take one or more of the older children with him on short trips by sail in and about Nova Scotia and the other Maritime Provinces.

He also continued his forays into steamboats. By 1828 the Halifax Steamboat Company had determined to build a steam ferry, fearful of losing its charter, which had been predicated upon such an initiative. The task of building this steamboat was given to Alexander Lyle in Dartmouth, and its keel was laid April 18, 1829. In a remarkable display of talent and workmanship, this, the first steamboat to be built in Nova Scotia, was constructed in just eight months. Lyle had had no prior experience in steamboat construction, but despite his unfamiliarity with the working drawings, and an engine that didn't arrive from England until November, the boat was still ready for launch on New Year's Day, 1830.

The Halifax Steamboat Company had come of age. Henceforth, steam would provide the power for the Halifax–Dartmouth ferries. The *Sir Charles Ogle*, as the ferry was christened, was named after Rear Admiral Sir Charles Ogle, baronet and commander of His Majesty's ships and vessels on the North American station.

Another interested observer and a friend of Cunard's, the newspaper editor Joseph Howe, reported favourably on the new steamboat, contrasting its performance with that of the old team boat: "The former boat seldom crossed we believe, in less than 20 minutes, and was often near an hour in making the passage—the present will glide over the harbour in seven minutes, making four passages within the hour. Her length of deck is 108 feet, width of beam 20 feet, width of deck 35 feet; she measures 176 tons and her engine is 30 horse power." The *Sir Charles Ogle* soon became a familiar feature of Halifax Harbour, giving over sixty years of continuous service before its retirement in 1890.

By 1830 there was another steamboat, the *Richard Smith*, on Nova Scotia waters. In August 1829 the keel was laid in Pictou for a steamboat purpose-built by the GMA to assist with the transportation of men and materials between the two mining operations in Pictou County and Cape Breton. Cunard was more than a casual observer throughout the construction and undoubtedly played a direct role in helping to secure engines and other components in England through the GMA offices. It took approximately twelve months to fit the boat out after launch; some say that it was plying the East River as early as July 1830.

On August 14, 1830, the *Richard Smith* made history when it became the first steam vessel to arrive in Sydney Harbour. Its inaugural trip to Sydney was by no means just show. Onboard were a number of miners brought to the Sydney coalfields to assist in raising coal to meet the great demand. Originally built for the sum of nine hundreds pounds sterling, the *Richard Smith*, which was later renamed the *Albion*, was a steady workhorse for the company until it was taken out of service about twelve years later.

With the dawn of a new decade and his children settled, Samuel was positioned to concentrate once again on his rapidly expanding business empire. He continued his active involvement in community and local affairs. His interests were many and diverse, but his motivation was invariably focused on public interest and commercial success. Not all of his business initiatives were successful — witness the canal and the whaling industry — but they were all entered into by Cunard with endless energy and single-mindedness of purpose.

In 1830, his high standing in the Halifax mercantile community resulted in Cunard's appointment to His Majesty's Council, the so-called Council of Twelve, which at that time exercised both executive and legislative functions. The council met at Government House on November 6, 1830, to induct Samuel into the group. Those in attendance included the lieutenant-governor, Sir Peregrine Maitland, Chief Justice Michael Wallace, Chàrles Morris, Mr. Justice Haliburton, Master of the Rolls, T. N. Jeffery, Enos Collins, H. N. Binney, and Samuel Cunard.

Thus another milestone was reached in the life of Samuel Cunard. At the age of forty-three he had attained the highest political standing in his native province. Henceforth he would be known as the Honourable Samuel Cunard. Joseph Howe, the newspaperman and politician who always maintained a cordial relationship with Cunard despite their political differences (among other things, Howe was an outspoken advocate of the eradication of His Majesty's Council), expressed the following sentiments in his newspaper about the appointment of Cunard to the Council:

> We hope the same liberal and expansive views which have distinguished Mr. Cunard as a merchant may be observable in his legislative character. He is wealthy and influential—he need fear no man, nor follow blindly any body of men; and we trust that he will not disappoint the hopes which many entertain of the benefit to be derived from his weight in the counsel of a branch, that at the present moment, is really in no good odour throughout the Province.

Cunard served faithfully, attending both legislative and executive meetings of council for the first few years of his appointment. He was also active on committees, motivated always by what he thought was best for business. This would inevitably lead him into conflict with Reformers, who were critical of and objected to a number of the councillors who, as prominent businessmen, they felt exercised too much influence and control at the expense of the public. As time passed much of this criticism was focused on those councillors, including Cunard, who were directors of the Halifax Banking Company. Cunard eventually stepped down from his position with the bank. He continued, however, to serve his community and province in the best way he knew: by furthering its economic growth.

CHAPTER 6

THE ROYAL WILLIAM

I t was 1830. There were now two steamships built in Nova Scotia and employed in the province. Samuel Cunard had been a keen participant in the projects; already he had acquired a vast amount of knowledge about the workings of steam engines, and now he had firsthand experience in their practical application to water transport. By this time, coastal steamships had appeared in other Maritime Provinces, a proliferation in the use of steam that further influenced Cunard's thoughts on the potential for applying steam on the North Atlantic. So significant was the advancement of steam in Nova Scotia that, at year-end, the Halifax press was inspired to write an account on the state of steam in the province:

We have said before that our native land, short four years ago, was a stranger to steam engines. Mark the rapid strides of advancement this powerful agent has made since, and is still making.

At the Albion Mines near Pictou is a drainage and lifting engine of 20 horse's power and a foundry engine which blows a cupola for melting iron, turns all kinds of lathes for boring and fitting machinery of 14 horse's power. A blast engine, with suitable blowing apparatus for three large blast furnaces, and a corresponding number of refineries etc. of 42 horse's power; two marine engines of upwards 50 horses each, ready to put into a steam boat, which we understand, is intended to ply between Pictou, Cape Breton, and Newfoundland; and a marine steam engine of 30 horse's power in a boat now at work between New Glasgow and the Town of Pictou; and to this list may be added two other large marine engine of 5 horse's each, intended to ply between Pictou and St. Peter's, and perhaps Arichat in Cape Breton, Prince Edward Island and Miramichi. Another engine, of 12 horse's power, to be employed in working a dredging boat, to clear away mud banks in rivers and wharves etc., and one or two others are spoken of to be erected in the Town of Pictou and New Glasgow to grind corn, card and spin wool, saw and turn timber etc., and for all which purposes steam power is admirably adapted.

At Cape Breton a drainage and draft engine has been erected this year on the Mines at Sydney of 30 horse's power, and we hear of another steam boat with an engine of 45 horse's power for that place, and to traverse the fine Lakes of the Bras d'Or, as well as a steam engine on the mines at Bridgeport, within an early period, of not less than 30 horses.

In this Town [Halifax] we have a 30 horse steam engine at work in our ferry boat, now upwards of twelve months which we are pleased to find has overcome the difficulties of salt in her boilers, and many other impediments natural to expect in the introduction of steam power into a new country. We learn with much satisfaction, the Steam Boat Company have ordered or shortly will order another steam engine of 16 horse's power, and thereby accommodate the public with a second boat to ply between the north end and Upper Dartmouth, so that if one happens to be out of repair, the public have another to look to.

We have troubled our readers with this account of the Steam Boat navigation that they may see the astonishing march of steam power into our rapidly rising colony. If, in the short space of four years, we are to witness 15 engines at work, consisting of 657 horses, what may we expect when the advantage of steam is more generally known and properly appreciated?

Steamboat activity continued unabated over the next few years, thus fuelling in Cunard what was rapidly becoming a preoccupation with steam. In 1831 the Nova Scotia legislature provided a grant to James Whitney of fifty pounds sterling for the construction of a larger steamboat to replace the St. John, in service between Saint John, New Brunswick, and Digby and Annapolis Royal in Nova Scotia. That vessel and its short-lived operation of just two years without any financial assistance proved that steam vessels required government subsidies in the form of mail contracts or outright aid to be commercially viable. The St. John had neither. Its successor was the SS *Henrietta*, which made tri-weekly trips between Saint John and Annapolis Royal, stopping at Digby and calling once or twice a week at Eastport, Maine.

In 1833, the *Maid of the Mist* established a weekly service between Saint John and Windsor, Nova Scotia. In 1836, the newly incorporated Annapolis Steam Boat Company built the 250-ton, 90-horsepower *Nova Scotia* for service between Saint John, Annapolis Royal, and Windsor. This was a large vessel, financed largely with New Brunswick capital. Other steamers followed, including the *Gazelle* and the *Royal Tar*, the latter being the first to become international in scope, offering a service between Saint John, Digby, Annapolis Royal, and Boston, Massachusetts.

Steam was taking hold throughout the colonies. However, as was still the case in England, all steamboats were virtually coastal vessels, built for use on inland waters or for relatively short crossings along coastal waters. The colonies were, nonetheless, urging England to consider steam to improve transatlantic communication and transportation.

The first substantial response to the prospect of employing steam on the North Atlantic had occurred in England in 1825, when the American and Colonial Steam Navigation Company petitioned the British government, setting forth the advantages of steam communication between Great Britain, Ireland, and Her Majesty's Dominions in North America. Regrettably for the principals of the company, their proposition for a transatlantic steamboat service did not succeed. Years of discussion and indecision on the part of government coupled with a lack of public confidence to invest in the scheme contributed to its demise. History would prove that the proposition was sound enough; the company was just ahead of its time. The British government would eventually accept the challenge, but not until fifteen years later.

The governments in Lower Canada and Nova Scotia, however, anticipated success for the transatlantic steamship service proposed by the American and Colonial Steam Navigation Company, and commenced negotiations for a steamboat that would run between Quebec and Halifax, connecting with the mail packets from Falmouth, England. In adverse winds and weather it often took sailing vessels three weeks to make the trip from Halifax to Quebec. As an incentive to generate interest, the legislature of Lower Canada that year offered 1,500 pounds sterling in three annual installments to anyone who would build a steamboat for this purpose. The Nova Scotia legislature also came forward, offering a subsidy of 250 pounds. It wasn't enough; no one responded, and much like the experience in England, the matter would remain in abeyance for a few years yet.

Samuel Cunard, however, was already busy formulating his plans to overcome the often-difficult passage up the St. Lawrence River. Based on what he had seen himself on the Bay of Fundy, where small steamboats now regularly traversed those turbulent waters, he was convinced that steam was the answer. As public clamour for steam increased, so did his conviction that the future was in steam. So, when government subsidies were doubled in 1830, he was ready to take a chance.

The original act of the legislature of Lower Canada of March 22, 1825, which had called for "the encouragement of the communication and more easy intercourse between the ports of Quebec and Halifax, and for the advancement of Navigation and the Trade between Canada and Nova Scotia," was repealed with a new act on

March 26, 1830. The goal of "sweetening the pot" was amply clear from the preamble of the new statute: "It is expedient that more effectual encouragement be offered for the establishment of an easy direct intercourse by means of steam vessels between this Province and the Province of Nova Scotia." The subsidy had now increased to three thousand pounds.

The new act and the doubling of the subsidy had the desired effect. In the intervening five years, interest in steam navigation had increased throughout the colonies. Samuel Cunard, with brothers Joseph and Henry, had expanded the base of operations of S. Cunard and Company throughout the Maritime Provinces and beyond to Newfoundland and Bermuda. They were three of some 235 shareholders from Quebec and the Maritimes who formed the Quebec and Halifax Steam Navigation Company in 1830. Shares were subscribed at twenty-five pounds each; the working capital was sixteen thousand pounds. The investors represented the leading merchants of the day, the great majority of whom were from Lower Canada. Most prominent among the Maritime investors was Samuel Cunard. He had been active in securing other shareholders in Halifax. A meeting of the subscribers for the promotion of the proposed steam navigation between Halifax and Quebec was held at the Exchange Coffee House in Halifax on March 11, 1830. There, a committee composed of Samuel Cunard, S. W. Deblois, and J. A. Creighton, previously appointed to solicit subscriptions, reported that 196 shares had been subscribed. In the business that followed, the seventy-six people present were asked to vote for one amongst them to be the agent representing the interests of the Nova Scotia shareholders with their Quebec counterparts. Samuel Cunard was their choice.

By the end of that month enough capital had been raised, and on March 31, 1830, an act to incorporate the Quebec and Halifax Steam Navigation Company was passed. What followed in the planning and construction of the first Canadian steamboat specifically designed to have ocean-going capabilities is a remarkable story of Canadian innovation and entrepreneurship.

No sooner was the steamboat company incorporated than a contract for the building of a steamship was given to John Saxton Campbell, merchant, and George Black, shipbuilder, both of Quebec. Moving at what today would be considered lightning speed, the keel of the new vessel was laid September 2, 1830, in the Black–Campbell shipyard at Cape Cove, under the cliff where Wolfe's Monument stands on the Plains of Abraham.

Building the *Royal William*, as the steamship was called, was no mean feat. Neither Campbell nor Black had any experience in building ocean-going steam vessels. They needed a specialist to design one for them. Their choice was a twenty-one-year-old by the name of James Goudie. He had recently served his apprenticeship in a shipyard in Greenock, Scotland, where he had worked on the design and construction of four steamers for service on the Irish Channel between Ireland and Scotland. His apprenticeship there had given him invaluable experience in designing an ocean-going ship. His talents were probably hereditary—his father had been involved in the building of the British naval fleet engaged on Lake Ontario in the War of 1812.

Not only was Goudie an excellent draftsman, but he must also have been an exceptional foreman. Work on the ship progressed at a rapid pace, especially given the workers' inexperience and lack of familiarity with the design and layout of a steamship. Work continued unabated throughout the winter until April, when the ship was ready for launching.

April 27, 1831, launch day, was an event the likes of which had never before been witnessed in Quebec. An immense crowd of thirty thousand crowded the shores of Cape Cove to witness Governor-General Lord Aylmer and Lady Aylmer christen the *Royal William*, named after the reigning monarch, William IV. Local press described the ship:

[She had a] magnificent appearance on the stocks, the prow, stern and quarter galleries are particularly tasteful...she went off beautifully amid cheers and firing of cannon, and when she floated looked a gallant ship. Mr. Black was the contractor; she is built with the greatest fidelity and strength, the sides forming a protection to the wheels against heavy seas. We have no doubt she will prove very fast. Her cost when ready for sea will be about 16,000 pounds.

The ship's official registration, dated August 22, 1831, describes the *Royal William* as a ship of 364 tons burthen that was 160 feet in length, 44 feet in breadth, and with draft of 17 feet and 9 inches. Schooner-rigged with three tall masts and standing bowsprit, the ship carried three square sails on the foremast. The wooden hull was carvel-built; the upper strakes of the hull were flared out, fore and aft, to envelop and protect the paddlewheels. The vessel carried a scroll head above its cut-water bow. It had one flush deck, and its square stern was decorated with mock quarters. The under-deck cabin is said to have been fitted out tastefully and to have contained some fifty berths. The dining saloon occupied the round house on deck. The ship allowed space for the accommodation of about eighty steerage passengers and thirty-six crew.

If the construction of the hull was remarkable, the fitting out of the ship following launch was equally so. On April 30, 1830, the *Royal William* proceeded to Montreal in tow of the *British America*, where its engines were installed by Bennett and Henderson Foundry at the foot of St. Mary's Current. The foundry had already acquired a good reputation for producing large, low-pressure marine steam engines. John Bennett, the senior partner, was born in Scotland and had served his apprenticeship with the Boulton and Watt, Soho Foundry in Birmingham, England, from where American steam pioneer Robert Fulton acquired the engine for the steamboat *Clermont* back in 1807.

The *Royal William's* engines had been made using the side lever principle, and were capable of developing about three hundred horsepower. The engines powered two paddlewheels, recessed into the hull halfway along the sides of the ship. They were each 18.5 feet in diameter and rotated at about twenty revolutions per minute. John Lowe, yet another Canadian who had recently completed his apprenticeship in Scotland, was employed by the foundry to oversee the installation of the machinery. The engines were successfully employed on the ship's return trip from Montreal to Quebec on August 13th, during which the Royal William steamed all the way, stopping in Sorel and Three Rivers en route.

Given his many business interests, it is unlikely that Cunard was present in Quebec for the launch of the *Royal William*. However, he soon had a first-hand look at his investment. The *Royal William* left Quebec with Captain John Jones on August 24, 1831, arriving in Halifax on August 31, having attained a maximum speed of thirteen knots along the way. The six-and-a-half days' passage time included a two-day stopover at Miramichi, where Joseph Cunard would have had an opportunity to appraise the new steamer—he was agent for the Quebec and Halifax Steam Navigation Company there.

The Halifax newspapers expressed the excitement felt in that city upon the arrival there of this magnificent steamship:

Quebec and Halifax Steam Ship arrived on Wednesday. The first official intelligence of her leaving Quebec was received last week of the Agent here [Cunard], and the 25th was named as the time of her starting. Correct as the stage coach, she left on the day appointed and arrived here just at the time expected by being six days in her passage. She remained two days at Miramichi, and, passing through the Straits of Northumberland on Monday night and Tuesday morning, arrived here on Wednesday forenoon. This speed is unprecedented under the most favourable of all former circumstances. The day of her arrival was very fine, and on intelligence of her appearance being communicated from the signal

station, considerable interest was exhibited by the inhabitants to obtain a view of their visitor. Some sought the house
tops, some the wharves, and others the surface of the harbour
in boats to gratify their curiosity. At ten o'clock she appeared
off Meagher's Beach, and, keeping under the western shore,
proceeded up the harbour in most majestic style. Several
guns and enthusiastic cheers welcomed her arrival and she
answered in a similar manner. Her beautiful fast sailing
appearance, the powerful and graceful manner in which her
paddles served to pace along, and the admirable command
her helmsman had over her, afforded a triumphant specimen
of what steam ships are.

One of those in Halifax most interested in this new marvel of steamboat engineering was, of course, Samuel Cunard. According to an
account written by J. G. Dentner, the second engineer aboard the
Royal William, the ship was repeatedly visited by Samuel Cunard in
Halifax. Cunard lost no opportunity to enquire about every particular regarding its speed, sea qualities, and consumption of fuel, carefully noting down all the information obtained, which "doubtless
enabled him to establish the magnificent fleet of ocean steamships
that still bear his name." While the latter observation is somewhat
speculative in nature, there is no doubt that Cunard spent considerable time aboard the steamer, literally taking notes on the three occasions it visited Halifax in the summer and fall of 1831, as well as the
Miramichi and Pictou.

Cunard exercised considerable control as agent for the Quebec
and Halifax Steam Navigation Company in Nova Scotia. None of
the company business in this province could be carried out except
through him. It was a position that afforded him the opportunity
to gain firsthand knowledge of both the construction and deployment of Canada's first ocean-going steamship. Equally important
was the regular contact and business dealings he had with the
Quebec shareholders of the company.

One of the many functions exercised by Cunard as agent was the securing of the annual government subsidy for the Quebec–Halifax service afforded by the *Royal William*. The first installment was given by warrant on November 4, 1831, by Lieutenant-Governor Sir Peregrine Maitland to "The Honourable Samuel Cunard, the Agent of the Quebec and Halifax Steam Boat Company, the sum of 500 pounds, being the annual amount grant as an encouragement for making a steam boat."

The original impetus for the construction of the *Royal William* was, of course, to improve communications between Lower Canada and the Maritime Provinces. It had a great start to its career, and every indication in 1831 was that it would meet the expectations of both its shareholders and the public. This was, however, not to be. 1832 proved to be a disaster for the ship and the company. Cholera, that dreaded disease, had arrived in Quebec. Three thousand people there were afflicted with the disease, and the *Royal William*, after inadvertently carrying some of those afflicted, was in quarantine for most of the season in Miramichi and Halifax. By the time the ship could secure a clean bill of health, it was late October and it went straight into winter quarters at Sorel.

During the winter and spring of 1832, while the *Royal William* wintered in Quebec, Cunard became increasingly concerned with company management. Correspondence between Cunard and the provincial secretary discloses something about the extent of his influence as company agent as well as his dissatisfaction with management of the Quebec and Halifax Steam Navigation Company. In a letter addressed to Sir Rupert D. George, provincial secretary, May 7, 1833, Cunard notes:

In reply to your communication regarding an application for the provincial grant for the Quebec & Halifax Steam Boat for the last (1832) year. I beg to state that I do not think the money should be paid in consequence of the boat's only making one trip (Quebec-Halifax) during the whole season. She was neglected in the winter and the frost burst the pipes and otherwise injured the machinery by which means a great expense was incurred and the sailing of the boat delayed until June 15th, whereas she should have made two or three trips before that period. This might have been guarded against by a little care on the part of the Committee (Quebec) and, having an Agent in pay, they can have no excuse for the neglect. They have already received 3975 pounds from this province the whole of which is lost by the management of the Quebec Committee, and the object in view, frustrated.

It is clear that Cunard did not share the commonly held view that the *Royal William's* abbreviated 1832 sailing schedule and resulting financial loss was due entirely to the interruption brought about by quarantine. He was quick to point out where he thought the fault lay. But by then it was too late. The losses incurred by the company were substantial; it could not meet its loan commitments, and in March 1833 the *Royal William* was put up for sale. On April 3, 1833, it was purchased by six of the mortgage holders and original shareholders for the sum of five thousand pounds, less than one-third the original cost of the ship, now just two years old.

The purchasers offered the other original shareholders the opportunity to buy back into a new company to own and operate the ship, but there was no response. It seems that the initial enthusiasm shared by the 235 subscribers had been lost during recent months with the abrupt turnaround in company fortunes. Included in those shareholders who lost their investment were Samuel, Joseph, and Henry Cunard.

The company had failed; and with it the high aspirations for a steamboat service joining Lower Canada to the Maritime Provinces. Public support and confidence in steamboat initiatives was shaken, making it difficult for Cunard to solicit financial support around Halifax a few years later for his grand steamboat venture. As for Cunard, the failure of management by committee would still be fresh in his mind when he set about structuring what would become the most famous of all steamboat companies.

The *Royal William*'s story was not over, however. In 1833, following the spring breakup of ice on the St. Lawrence, the *Royal William* was briefly used for pleasure excursions to Grosse Isle, and for towing on the river. Its new owners then arranged for a voyage to Boston, where, on June 17, it majestically entered the harbour, steaming past Fort Independence and firing a salute to the Stars and Stripes. It had just become the first sea-going steamer to fly the Union Jack in any US port.

Despite the warm reception in Boston, the Quebec owners decided to take the ship out of domestic service and put it up for sale across the Atlantic, in England. It was a decision that would place the *Royal William* and Samuel Cunard at the forefront of the evolution of ocean steam navigation.

Immediately upon arriving at Quebec on July 14, the *Royal William* was advertised for passage to England. Despite the modest fare of twenty pounds ("exclusive of wines"), the steamer left for Pictou, where she arrived on August 8, with only four cabin passengers aboard. There it took on coal and had some repairs done to its machinery while awaiting passengers from Prince Edward Island. Finally it was cleared, and on the August 18, 1833, steamed out of the Pictou harbour and into maritime history.

The voyage itself was not a moneymaker. With Captain John MacDougall at the helm, the ship departed Pictou with only seven passengers, thirty-six crew, and 254 chaldrons (or approximately 330 tons) of coal. Space aboard was at a premium, and priority was given to coal needed for the ship's engines. Captain MacDougall would later remark that leaving Pictou his ship was "deeply laden with coal, deeper in fact than I would ever attempt crossing the Atlantic with her again." Up to this point no one really knew how much coal would be required for a crossing of the North Atlantic. Skeptics had long argued that so much space would be required for coal as to make ocean transport impractical. The *Royal William* would soon prove that theory to be ill-founded. (Its remaining cargo — perhaps the most extraordinary to ever cross the Atlantic — consisted of a box of stuffed birds, six spars, one box, one trunk, household furniture, and a harp!)

The crossing proved to be quite eventful. The *Royal William* experienced a severe gale off the Grand Banks of Newfoundland, losing the head of its foremast and taking on water to such an extent that there was fear for a while that it might be sinking. The starboard engine became inoperable, which obliged Captain MacDougall to rely only on its port engine for ten days following the gale. Thereafter the weather abated and the ship continued across the Atlantic under steam, augmented by sail every fourth day, when the boilers had to be cleaned of salt. Salt water was still used in cooling the engines, producing an accumulation of salt, a situation corrected some years later with the patenting of a surface condenser that enabled marine boilers to be fed with freshwater and thus kept in constant operation.

The ship put into Cowes (Isle of Wight), England, for some repairs and to put a fresh coat of paint on the hull, enabling it to "go to London in fine style," where it arrived on September 12, 1833 — twenty-five days out from Pictou. The *Royal William* had become the first ocean steamer to cross the North Atlantic from west to east entirely under steam power.

(The *Royal William* was sold within a few weeks to a British ship owner for ten thousand pounds. It was eventually sold to the Spanish government and used as a warship under the name *Isabel Segunda*.)

Back home in Nova Scotia, Cunard, hearing of the safe arrival of the *Royal William* in London, was pleased but not surprised. He knew that the ship was built by competent marine architect James Goudie, and well-engined through the contribution of marine engineer Robert Napier. Cunard was already contemplating how he could employ the innovation and technology demonstrated by the *Royal William* in his own plans for the future. The ship would become the template for Cunard's first transatlantic steamer, still years away.

The experience with the *Royal William* was by no means Cunard's only steam project at the time. As a founder of the Halifax Steam Boat Company, Cunard had participated in the construction of Nova Scotia's first steamboat, and had since paid close attention to the *Sir Charles Ogle* as it regularly traversed the harbour between Halifax and Dartmouth. Within the next few years he assumed the presidency of the company and oversaw the construction of a second steam ferry, the *Boxer*. It was built and launched from the Lyle and Chappell Shipyard in Dartmouth in 1836.

In the meantime, Alexander Lyle had constructed a small, fifty-five-ton, schooner- rigged steam vessel. The *Pocahontas*, when launched in 1831, became the third steamer (after the *Sir Charles Ogle* and the *Richard Smith*) to be built in Nova Scotia, and the third local steam vessel in which Samuel Cunard had an interest. It was advertised for sale by auction shortly after its launch. Soon thereafter, its name appeared in the books of the General Mining Association, suggesting that the ship was purchased by the mining firm. Entries in the corporate records indicate that it was built at an initial cost of 1,437 pounds. By comparison, the *Richard Smith*, built a year earlier, cost 900 pounds.

Cunard initially used the *Pocahontas* to transport the mails between Halifax, Pictou, Charlottetown, and Miramichi, probably as a result of an agreement between himself and the GMA. It was eventually taken out of that service and operated by the GMA between the coalfields in Pictou County and Cape Breton.

The ship that took over the *Pocahontas*'s mails duties has a significant story of its own — and again, the GMA agency afforded Samuel the opportunity to further expand upon his working knowledge of steamboats. The GMA, either of its own volition or, more likely, in collaboration with Cunard, arranged for the construction of a steamboat in London, England, intended for use in the coal-mining operations in Nova Scotia. The *Cape Breton* was a schooner-rigged vessel of 124 tons, length of 105 feet, beam of 21 feet, and draft of 10 feet. Built by Benjamin Wallis and Company of Blackwall, England, in 1833, the ship played an important but little-known role in the evolution of steam navigation on the North Atlantic.

The *Royal William* departed Pictou, Nova Scotia on its fabled crossing of the Atlantic on August 18, 1833. On June 20, 1833, some two months earlier, the *Cape Breton* departed Plymouth, England, bound for Nova Scotia. It arrived in Sydney, Nova Scotia, on August 5, 1833, almost two weeks before the *Royal William* began its journey. The *Cape Breton* was berthed in Pictou the day *Royal William* embarked on its ocean crossing. The little steamer had taken forty-four days to make the trip across, suggesting that it probably sailed, and not steamed, its way over the ocean. However, it is likely that its engines were employed at least part of the time, and in that case, it was the first steamship to cross the North Atlantic from east to west.

Soon after arriving in Nova Scotia, the *Cape Breton* began transporting the mails around the Maritime Provinces. It was larger than the *Pocahontas* and better adapted to mail transport, especially in adverse weather conditions. For a number of years, the *Cape Breton* maintained a regular service carrying both mail and passengers between Pictou, Charlottetown, and Miramichi. In 1838 it was bought by Joseph Cunard and Company in Miramichi, becoming the first steam vessel to be owned by Cunard family interests. Joseph retained ownership of the *Cape Breton* until 1842, when the vessel returned to England, and was converted to a full-rigged ship by Robert Barclay of Glasgow, Scotland.

Despite all the other steam projects in Cunard's life at the time, the importance to his story of the crossing of the *Royal William* cannot be overstated. Although it did not establish any record for speed, the successful voyage of the *Royal William* disproved the theory that a steamer could not carry enough fuel to propel it across the ocean. This notion, had it not been disproved, might have delayed by much longer the bridging of the Atlantic with steam. Critics like the English scientist Dionysius Lardner, who long professed that "men might as well project a voyage to the moon as attempt steam navigation across the stormy Atlantic Ocean," were finally silenced. The *Royal William's* success convinced Cunard that steamers, properly built and staffed, could cross the North Atlantic with the regularity of steam engines on land—and without the great cost of building a railway over and around mountains and valleys. He would soon prove himself right.

CHAPTER 7

FROM MARITIME
MERCHANT
TO STEAM LION

I n the year 1833, Samuel Cunard, just forty-six years old, was
arguably the most prominent merchant in Nova Scotia. He had
amassed a fleet of more than seventy sailing ships, including
schooners, brigs, barques, and full-rigged ships. S. Cunard and
Company had prospered in the West Indian trade and an expanding
overseas British market. The Cunard wharves and warehouse off
Upper Water Street were constantly bustling with activity, despite
the depression conditions that beset Halifax at the time.

Cunard was still a widower and a single parent, but his mother-
in-law, Susannah Duffus, continued to help him immeasurably with
the raising of his young family. Edward, his eldest child, at eighteen,
had completed his formal schooling at King's College in Windsor,
Nova Scotia, and was demonstrating that he had a "head for business," as a junior partner in the family company. The rest of the children—Mary, age sixteen, Susan, fourteen, Margaret Ann, thirteen,
Sarah Jane, twelve, Anne Elizabeth, ten, William, eight, Isabella, six,
and Elizabeth, five—were all still at home on Brunswick Street in
Halifax under the loving care of Grandmother Duffus.

For Cunard, the days were not long enough; he was a man in constant motion, tending to a myriad of business interests that included shipping, shipbuilding, mail contracts, canals, banking, whaling, lighthouses, and government affairs, in addition to the responsibilities associated with his agency roles in the East India Company and the General Mining Association. Despite this inordinately heavy workload, Cunard still found time to devote to the affairs of his native city. He managed to participate as volunteer in the militia, where he was Captain in the Second Battalion of the Halifax Regiment; he was by then a long-time fire warden; he was an active member of the Nova Scotia Commercial Society and later President of the Chamber of Commerce; he was still assisting the poor and destitute immigrants in the city; he was a Halifax library benefactor; he was a member Halifax Mechanic's Institute; and he was a charter member of the Halifax Athenaeum.

His commercial empire, long since established in Nova Scotia, had spread to the other Maritime Provinces, New Brunswick and Prince Edward Island, east to Newfoundland, and south to Bermuda and the West Indies. He had established an enviable reputation for his firm and his name was well known in the Maritime business community. It was said that he successfully engaged in almost every kind of mercantile undertaking that promised advantage to himself or extended the commerce of the province. Despite having only a modest education, Cunard possessed natural business talents, quick perceptions, shrewd judgment, and an easy manner, which easily made him friends. In social and business circles he became acquainted with the military and the navy, especially the latter, by which means he was able to gain great influence with high-placed officials and nobility in England.

Unlike many of his contemporaries, Cunard was very much a hands-on businessman. He enjoyed nothing more than sailing aboard his own vessels whenever the occasion arose. Given the nature of his business he had ample opportunity to sail about the Maritime Provinces and to cross the Atlantic Ocean. In this way he was able to gain firsthand experience with wind, weather, and water conditions. Perhaps more importantly, he learned how both vessels and crews performed in all manner of conditions. And time spent during coastal cruising or ocean crossings, while arduous by today's standards, was never wasted. When he wasn't on the bridge, Cunard could be found in his stateroom-turned-office, fomenting plans for his next venture or attending to his correspondence.

Throughout his career, Cunard shunned public speaking; he was a man of few spoken words. However, what he lacked in oratorical style and ability, he more than made up for in writing etiquette. Cunard had a writing style that reflected his own personality. He wrote what he thought. He did not mince or waste words. His letters were precise, handwritten renderings of his thoughts on a given subject — written with such honesty and openness that they still read as if the man were present, in person, speaking to his correspondent.

Sadly, very few of the thousands of letters written by Cunard have survived. The corporate records of A. Cunard and Son as well as S. Cunard and Company, covering Cunard's early business career in Nova Scotia during the period 1812–1840, were destroyed when the Cunard warehouse and offices on Upper Water Street were demolished in 1917. It is reported that a large pallor of smoke hung over the Cunard wharves for weeks while the files and records of the Cunard businesses were removed and burned before the ironstone warehouse was dismantled. Halifax lost a fine example of nineteenth century architecture and, with it, irreplaceable records of this period of our maritime history.

Fortunately some pieces of Cunard's correspondence have survived time and the ravages of progress. Some were written while Cunard was agent for the General Mining Association and relate to the GMA's mining operations in Cape Breton and Pictou County. A few have been carefully preserved at the Beaton Institute of Cape Breton University, in Sydney, Nova Scotia. A look at a series of letters between Cunard, as the GMA's agent in Halifax, and Henry Poole, mine manager at the Bridgeport Mine in Cape Breton, provide insight into Cunard's character and management style.

> The amount heretofore kept on your books in my name will in future be appended 'Halifax Agency'. Look into your stock of coal and all other things and advise me from time to time what you want and your requests shall be attended to. Whenever you can be useful to Mr. Brown [the Cape Breton Mines manager] in giving explanations or otherwise. I am sure you will do so—and let me beg of you to give your best attention to all things. You will find Mr. Brown and me always ready and willing to assist you. Be up in the morning as early as the workmen, and show them that you are on the alert—all things find their way to your employees and if you are attentive, it will in the end be to your advantage.
> *(Samuel Cunard to Henry Poole, July 25, 1838)*

> You must be aware that if any loss should arise for the want of such information, you would be much blamed.
> *(Samuel Cunard to Henry Poole, August 1, 1838. Cunard had been receiving less-than-complete information on various accounts from his mine manager, and in this three page letter counsels Poole on the consequences of this type of accounting practice.)*

> I have received your letter of July 31. I am confident that everything will go on well under your management and as my credit as well as your own is at stake, it will be an additional motive for exertion on your part. I have assured the Board of your capability and devotion.
> *(Samuel Cunard to Henry Poole, August 8, 1838)*

> I propose going to England in the Packet. If I can be useful to you in any way, I am sure you will believe me when I say it will afford me my sincere pleasure to be so.

(Samuel Cunard to Henry Poole, January 9, 1839).

I have your letter of 1 instant. Do everything in your power to keep the affairs of the Association on a good and regular basis — and raise all the coal you can at as little cost as possible. This will be the best mode of recommending yourself to the consideration of the Board. I leave in the Packet and if you have anything that you would like to communicate, drop me a line by the next packet. I shall return very soon by the way of the States.

(Samuel Cunard to Henry Poole, January 16, 1839).

Cunard's letters provide insight into the manner in which he arranged for his many business interests to be carried on when he was necessarily absent from the province. Those absences were becoming more frequent and of longer duration. To compensate, family members were integrated into the Cunard business. Younger brothers Joseph and Henry had long since been set up in business in New Brunswick. For the past number of years Samuel had been gradually introducing his eldest son, Edward, into the family business; the latter would regularly travel, and like his father demonstrated an inclination for business at a very early age. In 1839, at just twenty-four, Edward had proven himself to be capable of running the Halifax operations of S. Cunard and Company while his father was away. This must have given considerable comfort to his father, who knew that if all of his business plans came to fruition, his time would be at a premium.

This series of letters has further significance. It arose out of a very formative period of Cunard's career, at a moment when his life and maritime history was about to change forever.

In the last letter of the group, Cunard indicates that he is soon to "leave in the Packet," referring to the sailing packets that crossed the Atlantic with passengers and the mails from Europe to the colonies. The trip still typically took up to six weeks, depending on the weather. This particular voyage Cunard speaks of was no ordinary trip, for, just a few weeks previously, Cunard had learned of a call for tenders by the British Admiralty for the regular transport of the mails across the North Atlantic by steamship — to replace the irregular and uncertain schedules of the Falmouth Packets. On this crossing, Samuel Cunard travelled to England for the purpose of negotiating for the transatlantic steam mail service.

But despite what must have been an overwhelming preoccupation with plans for the trip to London, Cunard first tended to his work commitments at home. His communications with Henry Poole reveal something of Cunard's unswerving loyalty and attention to the affairs of the GMA, even as he was about to embark on the greatest challenge of his life.

The British Admiralty advertised for tenders to carry the mails by steam from England to New York via Halifax on November 7, 1838. The time was right. In Nova Scotia politicians and press had been speaking out strongly in support of a steamship link between England and the colonies for some time. Ever since the War of 1812, Nova Scotian merchants and politicians had been striving to maintain a monopoly on trade with the West Indies and to bolster trade with United States. But in 1830 the Americans obtained direct access to those islands, and Nova Scotians soon found that the unwanted American competition with the shorter haul and larger supply soon had a serious negative impact on their business. It was not long before they directed their dissatisfaction towards England. They began to constantly petition the British government to make more adequate provision for the conveyance of mail, to protect their political and economic interests and to incorporate them more closely in the Empire to offset the rival attractions of their competent and aggressive neighbours to the south. Similar exhortations were regularly appearing in the press, on the floor of the local legislature, and in the writings of local authors, to great effect.

In Britain, maritime merchants had been quick to perceive the importance of steam and the practical demonstration in 1833 by the *Royal William* of its potential for transatlantic travel. In the years immediately following, the commercial sector in Britain experienced a groundswell of interest in steam and its potential for accelerating the processes of international finance between it and America. Companies were established with the express purpose of building vessels with which to institute a transatlantic steamship service. While the British and American Steam Navigation Company (not to be confused with the British and North American Royal Mail Steam Packet Company, to come) was building the *British Queen,* another new enterprise, also in Bristol and known as the Great Western Steamship Company, built and launched the steamer *Great Western.* It and yet another steamer, the *Sirius,* built by the St. George Steam Packet Company, crossed the Atlantic in April of 1838, arriving in New York within hours of each other. A few days later the *Sirius* played an even more important part in the evolution of ocean steam navigation.

Shortly after the British steamer *Sirius* had arrived in New York, a group of highly respected and influential Nova Scotia businessmen was en route to England aboard the sailing vessel *Tyrian.* Joseph Howe, the prominent Halifax journalist and politician, Thomas Chandler Haliburton, a Supreme Court Judge and renowned author (he penned the famous "Sam Slick" tales), and Charles Fairbanks, a Halifax barrister and former director, with Cunard, of the Halifax Steam Boat Company, were all on board. The *Tyrian* became becalmed in the Atlantic, and as it drifted in the water, waiting for a wind to take it to England, it was soon overtaken by the steamer *Sirius* on its return voyage to Cork, Ireland. The *Sirius* came alongside the *Tyrian* and took its mail, as it was likely to reach its destination days and possibly weeks before the much slower sailing vessel. Howe and his friends crossed over to the *Sirius* with the mail bags and shared a glass of champagne with its commander, Lieutenant Roberts, R. N., in his cabin.

This chance encounter had profound influence upon Joseph Howe and his business associates. As Howe later wrote:

> Never did we feel so forcibly the contrast between the steamer and the sailing vessel, even for the deep sea passage. The difference is hardly greater between poetry and mathematics. We rowed back to the *Tyrian*, gratified perhaps that we had been the first passengers that had boarded on the high seas the first steamer that had made the voyage from Britain to America and back, but not at all pleased with the prospect of being left behind to the tender mercies of wind and canvas, when a few tons of coal would have done the business much better.

Thereafter Howe, with his considerable influence, pressed for action in Britain to establish a steam link across the Atlantic. In his mind there was no topic of any more importance and he exhorted the newly formed chamber of commerce in Halifax to direct its energies and intelligence to this initiative.

During the summer of 1838 Howe and representatives from New Brunswick returned to London to press their cause. The Crane–Howe Memorandum, drafted by Joseph Howe, was presented to Lord Glenelg at the Colonial Office on August 24, 1838. In it the petitioners stressed that:

> If Great Britain is to maintain her footing upon the North American continent—if she is to hold the command of the extensive sea coast from Maine to Labrador, skirting millions of square miles of fertile lands, intersected by navigable rivers, indented by the best harbours in the world containing now a million and a half people and capable of supporting many millions, of whose aid in war and consumption in peace she is secure—she must, at any hazard of even increased expenditure for a time, establish such a line of rapid communication by steam, as will ensure the speedy transmission of public dis-

patches, commercial correspondence and general information through channels exclusively British, and inferior to none in security and expedition. The pride as well as the interests of the British people would seem to require means of communication with each other, second to none which are enjoyed by other states.

The memorandum reflected the collective yearnings of all Nova Scotians at the time, and it struck a chord in Britain. Within a few months the British government called for tenders for steam communication between England and America via Halifax.

Samuel Cunard nearly missed the tender call. Ironically, by the time the English mails arrived in Halifax from Britain by sail packet, the time for responding to the tender had passed. Anyone else might have been deterred by the now-past deadline and conceded that it was too late to act. Cunard, however, was unfazed. He suspected that his British competition, whoever they might be, could not meet the terms of the tender. He promptly boarded a packet and set sail for England to present his case.

He didn't go unprepared. He had been methodically preparing for this eventuality for many years. When Joseph Howe had finally arrived in London aboard the *Tyrian* in May 1838, he had gone immediately to see his friend Samuel Cunard — who was in the country on business — at his hotel at 206 Piccadilly, where they engaged in conversation about the prospects for steam. Cunard and his son William left for home the next day. By the time the packet reached Halifax a month later Cunard had already decided to try and raise capital to build three or four large passenger steamers himself for a transatlantic service.

He spent much of the summer of 1838 trying to raise working capital for a private ocean steam packet company of his own initiative. He first approached business associates in Halifax, but quickly found that few were prepared to risk such an investment. He was encouraged to forget such a far-fetched scheme; perhaps the fairly recent financial failure of the *Royal William* venture was still fresh in their minds. Undaunted, Cunard went to Boston to try to drum up interest. There he found merchants and ship owners of the view that steamers were an impractical, dangerous novelty. They preferred to invest in American sailing packets and ocean windjammers. Cunard could find neither interest nor capital in Boston. He returned to Halifax with a new plan: he would obtain financing in England, where there was a renewed interest in ocean steamships.

Cunard now looked to his friends in government and the Admiralty to help in his quest for the mail contract. The first person he engaged was the lieutenant-governor of Nova Scotia. Amongst his papers when he departed Halifax for London in January 1839 was a letter of introduction addressed to Lord Glenelg of the colonial office from Sir Colin Campbell, in which Campbell wrote:

> This will be presented to you by the Honourable Samuel Cunard, one of the Executive Council; of this Province who proceed to England by the packet. He has requested an introduction to your Lordship which I have much pleasure in giving him as I have always found him one of the firmest supporters of the government. His being one of the principal bankers and merchants and Agent of the General Mining Association and also Commissioner of Lighthouses gives him a good deal of influence in this community.

The lengthy crossing of the Atlantic by sail gave Cunard more time to work out details of his approach to the British Admiralty tender call. Arriving in London in February, he immediately got in touch with James C. Melvill, the secretary of the Honourable East India Company, on whose behalf Cunard acted as agent in Halifax. Cunard's first objective was to secure a shipbuilder and a contract for construction of the steam vessels he contemplated for the Atlantic service. His friend Melvill recommended the Glasgow firm of Wood and Napier. Robert Napier, the head of the firm and purportedly the best marine engineer in Britain, had designed the engines for the British Queen. Cunard did not approach Napier himself, choosing rather to make contact through another influential friend.

From his GMA office at Ludgate Hill in London, Cunard wrote to William Kidston, an acquaintance he had made in Halifax and the head of the venerable Glasgow mercantile firm of Messrs. William Kidston and Sons. Cunard asked Kidston to approach Napier on his behalf. This was done and, following an exchange of letters in which he matter-of-factly stated his requirements for steamers, Cunard met with Napier at his home, Lancefield House in Glasgow. Their talks were successful and by March 18, 1839, Cunard had secured a contract from Napier for the construction of three steamers of 960 tons at a cost of thirty-two thousand pounds each. A fourth steamer would later be added to that number.

With the contract for the steamers in hand, Cunard moved on to address the mail contract with the British Admiralty. These dealings were with his friend Sir Edward Parry and bore fruit. In 1837 Parry was made comptroller of steam machinery and the packet service, with the task of converting the old sailing packets to steam. Parry had become a good friend of Cunard's while stationed with the Royal Navy in Halifax some twenty years earlier, and that friendship would now prove a real asset to Cunard.

The mail contract, under which Cunard was to receive an annual payment of fifty-five thousand pounds for the service, was signed on May 4, 1839. Cunard had now secured both the mail contract and the agreement for the construction of his ships before having raised any money to pay for them! The next hurdle, raising the capital, would be a further test of his powers of persuasion and diplomacy.

Cunard moved quickly. With little encouragement in either London or Liverpool to finance his project for a transatlantic shipping company, he went back to Glasgow and met again with Robert Napier. It was a wise decision. Napier was a good friend of George Burns, also of Glasgow, who, together with his brother James, had been running a small fleet of coastal steamers to Liverpool. The

Burnses in turn had competition — the MacIver brothers, David and Charles, in Liverpool. Napier believed that they might be prepared to invest in Cunard's enterprise if Cunard was to offer the Liverpool agency for his ships to the MacIver brothers and the Glasgow agency to the Burns brothers. The strategy worked and on May 14, 1839, George Burns and David MacIver agreed to join forces as investors in Cunard's venture.

It was a year before all the paperwork was concluded, but by May 1840 all the documentation was in place. The result was a partnership with initial capital of 270,000 pounds. This was later increased to 300,000 pounds, subscribed by some thirty-three investors. The original principals, Napier, Burns, and MacIver, had been very successful in attracting others to invest. Indeed, so persuasive were they that investor William Connal, the head of a large firm engaged in the commission trade, when approached by George Burns, responded: "I know nothing of steam navigation, but if you think well of it, I'll join you."

The British and North America Royal Mail Steam Packet Company, later referred to as Mr. Cunard's Line, and later still, the Cunard Line, was born. Samuel Cunard was the largest of the thirty-three subscribers, holding 550 of the original 270,000 shares, valued at 55,000 pounds. The other principal partners who directed the affairs of the company with Cunard had much smaller shareholdings. Robert Napier had 61 shares, James Burns, 51, George Burns, 55, and David and Charles MacIver, 40 each.

Samuel Cunard had accomplished what no one on either side of the Atlantic had been able to do. His eight months in England from January to August 1839 had produced spectacular results. During that space of time the "quiet colonial" from Halifax had found a builder and secured a contract for the construction of four ocean-going steamships, negotiated a mail contract with the British Admiralty, and then brought the whole initiative together with a group of highly respected and influential businessmen, previously unknown to him, in the formation of the British and North American

Royal Mail Steam Packet Company. Cunard's quest for an "ocean railway" was finally within reach.

Back home in Nova Scotia, Cunard's triumph was hailed by all political parties and the press. Suddenly there were prospects for Halifax and the British colonies that excited the imaginations of Nova Scotians. The *Nova Scotian* sang Cunard's praises, rejoicing that "a colonist, whose enterprising spirit we have often had occasion to notice, has had the courage to grapple with an undertaking so vast as the carriage of mails by steam between Halifax and the Mother Country — Halifax and Boston — and Pictou and Quebec."

Samuel arrived home from England in August 1839 and was greeted with high praise and commendation by Haligonians. His brother Joseph, who had returned to Halifax from England some months previously, had already spread the word in Halifax about his brother's successful bid for the mail contract, even though the deal had not been finalized at that time.

Quite the opposite of his younger brother, Samuel shunned rather than sought public attention. Halifax, however, was not about to let his great achievement pass unnoticed. On August 23 a committee met Cunard at his home on Brunswick Street, presenting a congratulatory address and announcing arrangements for a public meeting and dinner to be held in his honour at McNab's Island in Halifax Harbour. On August 28, 1839, the appointed day for the picnic, the ferry *Sir Charles Ogle* transported Cunard and guests to the island. It was a festive event culminating with a dinner held in great style. Many toasts were given, the most poignant given to the guest of honour: "The Honourable Samuel Cunard — our pride as a Townsman — our admiration as a merchant – may every success attend his establishment of Steam Navigation across the Atlantic." Cunard's response was characteristically brief and overtly modest. He gave all the credit for the mail contract to the British government, conceding at the same time that he had managed to convince the Admiralty that biweekly sailings were vital, as the monthly service proposed by Britain would "still have left the British colonies behind an age."

Cunard had no time to rest on his laurels. In May, while he had been in England negotiating his mail contract, work had been progressing at the Albion Mine in Pictou County on a new steel rail line. Three steam locomotives, the Samson, the Hercules, and the John Buddle, had arrived in the spring from Newcastle Upon Tyne aboard the brig *Ytham*. They were landed at Pictou and brought up the East River in lighters, in the tow of the GMA steamboat *Richard Smith*, which had been renamed the *Albion*. Early in September, Cunard went to Pictou to make arrangements for port facilities for the new steamship service, shortly after which members of his family joined him at Mount Rundle, mine manager Richard Smith's home, in celebrating the opening of the new GMA railroad. It was a six-mile length of double narrow-gauge steel that ran from the Albion Mine to the loading grounds at Abercombie Point, near the mouth of the East River.

The Albion Railway was a remarkable feat of engineering. Work had begun in 1836 under the guidance of Peter Crerar from Breadalbane, Scotland, and was completed in 1839 at a cost of 160,000 dollars. The new railway was in every way equal to England's first steam railway. The Samson was the first of the three engines to be placed on the track and therefore was the first steam locomotive to run on steel rails in British North America. It has been preserved and is a major attraction in the collection of the Museum of Industry at Stellarton, Nova Scotia.

Many celebrations marked the opening of the line. The company steamers *Pocahontas* and *Albion* brought some one thousand people on lighters from Pictou to New Glasgow via the East River. From there they were taken by train, hauled by the new steam locomotive Hercules six miles on the new rail line to the Albion Mine, now Stellarton, where thousands gathered. Processions were formed of the various trades, the Masonic Lodges, and the Pictou Volunteer Artillery Company. Bands, pipers and banners were everywhere. Wagons, fitted for passengers, were attached to the steam locomotives and shunted back and forth to New Glasgow, "giving a new sensation to multitudes." Employees of the company were then treated to a feast supplemented by eleven hundred pounds of beef and mutton and corresponding quantities of rum.

In the evening a dinner party was held for invited guests in the new stone engine house where the locomotives were to be kept. The head table was decorated with a miniature railroad track along which a model train carried the wine decanters. Samuel Cunard — the agent for the company, so recently returned from his success in England — although neither the designer nor builder of the new rail line, was nonetheless the focus of everyone's attention. Cunard steamers were soon to be arriving like clockwork at Halifax, and all present rejoiced with the knowledge that the steamers' bunkers would be filled with GMA coal.

As for Samuel Cunard, the so-called Steam Lion, his thoughts were already focused on his next challenge — ensuring that his quartet of ocean steamers, now under construction in Scotland, would be ready to join his new transatlantic service six months hence.

CHAPTER 8

THE *BRITANNIA*
RULES THE WAVES

C unard's contract with the British Admiralty provided for the carriage of mails with all possible speed from Liverpool to Halifax and from thence to Boston. In addition, Cunard agreed to provide a service to Quebec during those months when the St. Lawrence River was open to shipping, with the port of Pictou on Nova Scotia's Northumberland Strait being the departure point. He had a separate contract with the Nova Scotia government for the carriage of those mails overland from Halifax to Pictou. The steamboats to be employed on the Pictou and Boston routes were to be of 150 horsepower, or just half that of the larger steamers contemplated for the transatlantic route.

To address the short haul routes, and while the first of his Atlantic steamships were being built in Scotland by his new partner, Robert Napier, Cunard set out to find a steam vessel that would be suitable for the Pictou–Quebec service. He settled upon the seven-hundred-ton paddle steamer *Unicorn*, which had been built in 1836 as a coastal steamer traveling between Glasgow and Liverpool for Cunard's other newfound partners, George and James Burns. The partnership was already paying dividends. The deal was struck and the *Unicorn* became the first steamship in Samuel Cunard's fleet.

It was a handsome vessel. The *Unicorn* was built of wood as a three-masted schooner by Robert Steele and Company of Greenock, Scotland. With a length of 163 feet, it was powered by two side lever engines and had a beautiful bowsprit on which it carried a figurehead in the form of its namesake. The stern was square and decorated with mock quarters. Incorporating the latest in steam technology, its low pressure boilers were freshwater fed, doing away with the vexing problem of "salting up of the boilers," which had plagued the *Royal William* and other early steam vessels.

On May 16, 1840, it set out from Liverpool on its first transatlantic crossing to Halifax. Cunard carefully chose Captain Walter Douglas for this command. Douglas had gained considerable experience working with steamboats on the St. Lawrence River as far back as 1825. Prior to taking command of the *Unicorn* he was master of the Canadian government ship *Culinare*, which had been engaged in surveying of the St. Lawrence River. Aboard for this historic trip were twenty-seven passengers, including Samuel's son Edward, who now was now established as the company's representative in Halifax.

Despite a rough crossing, the *Unicorn* arrived safe and sound at Halifax on June 1, 1840. People there turned out in great numbers to witness its arrival. Civic leaders met the ship upon docking at the Cunard wharves. Speeches were given; praise was heaped upon the Cunard enterprise, and Edward Cunard was the recipient of the goodwill of his townsfolk. He was joined aboard by other members of both the Cunard and Duffus families who took advantage of the spare cabins to make the voyage and share the excitement of the reception in Boston, where the *Unicorn* arrived on June 3.

Boston, forewarned of the *Unicorn*'s arrival, was ready and waiting to celebrate. Ships in the harbour were decked out with flags, bands played, church bells rang, and the Union Jack flew from flagpoles all over the city. Newspapers all over Massachusetts carried front pages devoted to the arrival of the *Unicorn* and the great blessings the Cunard Line was to confer upon Boston. Edward Cunard was guest of honour at a large civic banquet three days later to celebrate the opening of steam navigation between the Kingdom of Great Britain and Boston, and Captain Douglas and the officers of the *Unicorn* were feted. Mayor Jonathan Chapman hosted the event and was joined by the leading officials and merchants of the town. The premier toast of the night was reserved for Samuel Cunard, though he was not present, and was made by Edward Everett, one of the nation's greatest orators: "The Honourable Samuel Cunard — the founder of the direct steam navigation between Great Britain and the City of Boston — a wise negotiator — while governments are arguing about boundaries [as Britain and the United States were at that time], he makes a successful incursion with a peaceful force, into the heart of the country." Henry Wadsworth Longfellow, one of the 450 invited guests, offered these words: "Steamships! The pillar of fire by night and the cloud by day, which guide the wanderer over the sea."

If the reception given to the first steamship of the Cunard Line in Halifax and Boston was to be judged by today's standards, Samuel Cunard would be considered a marketing genius. The decision to send the *Unicorn* across the Atlantic in advance of the new steamships being built more than achieved the goal of attracting public attention to the steamboat venture. For the next four years *Unicorn* would give fortnightly service between Pictou and Quebec before being repositioned to Newfoundland.

Meanwhile, Samuel Cunard had been busy in Britain overseeing the construction of his Atlantic steamboats. While in London, he worked out of the offices of the General Mining Association at Ludgate Hill. It was from there that on February 25, 1839, he wrote Messrs. William Kidston and Sons, Glasgow, seeking their assistance in obtaining estimates from Wood and Robert Napier for steamboats of different size and horsepower. What was made abundantly clear from his correspondence was Cunard's wish for quality, and not extravagance in his ships.

I am told that Messrs. Wood and Napier are highly respectable builders, and likely to be enabled to fulfill any engagement they may enter into...I am told that the *London* is a fine vessel, and about the description of vessel that I might require, but I have not seen her. I shall want these vessels to be of the very best description, and to pass a thorough inspection and examination of the Admiralty. I want a plain and comfortable boat, not the least unnecessary expense for show. I prefer plain work in the cabin, and it will save a large amount in the cost.

After entering into negotiations with Cunard for the construction of his steamboats, Napier recommended that the size of the vessels be increased. Increasing the size of course inflated the costs; however, Cunard was not deterred, and after weighing Napier's advice, wrote to the Scottish builder:

Since I left you this morning I have thought a good deal of your recommendation to add a little to the size of the boats, more especially as you were so good as to say you would give me the additional power. I feel confident the boats would be much improved and I will thank you to ask Mr. Wood what additional sum he will charge for adding ten feet to the length and one foot to the breadth. I think he will not be unreasonable with me. I want to show the Americans what can be done in Glasgow and that neither Bristol or London boats can beat them.

These few succinct sentences portray Cunard as a decisive business-man who wasn't averse to infusing a little nationalism into the contract talks in an effort to extract a fair bargain.

His efforts succeeded. Within a few weeks agreement was reached between Cunard and Napier for the construction of larger vessels. As Napier wrote to James C. Melvill on March 19, 1839:

I am of the opinion that Mr. Cunard has got a good contract, and that he will make a good thing of it. From the frank, off-hand manner in which he contracted with me, I have given him the vessels cheap, and I am certain they will be good and very strong ships.

At the same time Cunard wrote Napier from London to advise that the Admiralty and Treasury were highly pleased with the size of the boats: "I have given credit where it is due to you and Mr. Wood. I have pledged myself that they shall be the finest and best boats ever built in this country." Cunard had set the bar high, and, as if that were not enough, he then subtly brought further pressure to bear and challenged his builders by concluding his letter: "You have no idea of the prejudice of some of our English builders. I have had several offers from Liverpool and this place, and when I have replied that I have contracted in Scotland, they invariably say 'you will neither have substantial work nor completed on time.'" Napier and Wood soon proved the skeptics wrong, as was doubtless Cunard's intent.

Throughout these months, when construction details and scheduling for the world's first transatlantic steamship service occupied his every waking hour, Cunard still found time to keep in touch with his family back home in Nova Scotia. He remained very much the father to his children, despite intense business pressures. A letter written to his daughter Mary in Charlottetown on April 4, 1839, underlines the close relationship Cunard maintained with his children:

My Dear Mary…I expected before this time to have been on my way home, but here I am, still likely to remain for a month at least. I had to go to Scotland to contract for the building of my Steam Boats and shall have to pay another visit to see how they are progressing. They will be beautiful vessels, quite equal to any ever built and I think, much superior. They will be nearly double the size and power of the *Media* and will go two miles per hour faster.

Then, on a much more personal note, Cunard informed his daughter that he hasn't forgotten her shopping list:

> I have ordered all the articles you mentioned to me and if I see any little thing that I think would please you I will add it to the list.

Cunard was in London throughout the winter and spring of 1840 so he could keep a close watch over the construction of his steamships. The ship upon which he was most focused was of course the *Britannia,* his flagship. When he wasn't on site at the shipyard, Cunard continued regular communication by post with Robert Napier. As work neared completion he wrote to Napier on June 13, 1840: "I am happy to learn from you that steam is up in *Britannia* and the machinery working well—though I never doubted on this head, but it is very satisfactory to know that all is right. I am anxious to have the report of her sailing which I hope to get on Monday."

The first of the four steamers contracted, the *Britannia* was launched at Glasgow, Scotland, on February 5, 1840. As its elegant wooden hull slid into the welcoming waters of the Clyde River, the *Britannia* became the first in a long succession of liners that have proudly borne—and still bear—the name Cunard.

The *Britannia,* although built plain in accordance with Cunard's wishes, was still a graceful vessel. It was 207 feet long, carried a beam of 34 feet, and was bark-rigged, with fore and aft rigging on the mizzenmast and square rigging on the mainmast and foremast. It had a beautiful clipper bow replete, under the bowsprit, with a bronze figurehead of Britannia carrying a trident. Its stern was square and it sported a tall red funnel amidships and two huge paddlewheels. It was capable of carrying six hundred tons of coal to feed three furnaces that would drive the ship along at a steady eight and a half knots. A stone statue of Britannia sits today atop the provincial building in Halifax.

After nearly five months of fitting out, by early July, the *Britannia* was ready for its historic voyage. Too large to be loaded at dockside in Liverpool, it was moored in the Mersey River with both passengers and mail loaded aboard by tender. The *Britannia*, first flagship and prototype of the Cunard fleet, steamed out of the Mersey on July 4, 1840, a date that due to both accident and shrewd marketing, would often later be recognized by the company for launchings and other milestones. Some thought it to be a good omen for the future of the service to the United States. In fact, original plans were for the *Britannia* to have departed Liverpool on July 2. The two-day delay was brought about by further adjustments to its machinery before setting forth on its history-making voyage.

Among the sixty passengers and ninety-three crew was the founder, Samuel Cunard. This was his crowning moment, and to share it with him was his daughter Anne, then seventeen years of age, and her friend Laura Haliburton. Laura was a daughter of Justice Thomas Chandler Haliburton from Windsor, Nova Scotia, the humourist who had been aboard the becalmed *Tyrian* with Joseph Howe. (Years later the two girls would become sisters-in-law when Laura wed Anne's brother William.) Other notable passengers included the Lord Bishop of Nova Scotia, two American consuls, and the Earl of Caledon, as well as businessmen from Upper and Lower Canada, the British colonies, and the New England states.

The transatlantic crossing was made without incident. The master, Lieutenant Henry Woodruff, had been handpicked to be captain. He and the entire crew performed admirably on the voyage, earning the praise and adulation of those aboard.

The most interested passenger aboard the *Britannia* was, of course, Samuel Cunard. Crossing the North Atlantic was nothing new to him. He had done so many times, often on his own sailing ships. He had always been a hands-on ship owner, taking every opportunity to sail aboard his vessels. This crossing was different, however—Cunard traversed the Atlantic from Liverpool, England, to Halifax, Nova Scotia, under steam in just twelve and a half days, compared to the twelve or more weeks a journey by sail could take, and was making history with every passing moment and each nautical mile. The ship's engines and machinery performed flawlessly, driving the stout vessel along through sometimes-rough seas and against strong head winds at a constant speed of eight and a half knots. Samuel Cunard lived his dream of providing the world with its first ocean railway.

Meanwhile, the *Unicorn* was berthed at the Cunard wharves in Halifax, in readiness to transport mail and passengers from the *Britannia* to Quebec. The city anxiously awaited the arrival of the Cunard flagship. No one knew however exactly when to expect it, nor could anyone have anyway of determining when it might make port. As it turned out, the *Britannia* arrived at two in the morning on July 17. A cannon shot had been the agreed signal if the *Britannia* arrived after dark, but the *Britannia* was berthed at the Cunard wharf for some hours before the shot was sounded because no one had informed the signalman of its arrival!

At dawn people thronged to the waterfront to get a glimpse of the steamer. The welcoming committee, complete with rehearsed speeches, arrived dockside to a scene of considerable activity. Cargo, including mail, was being taken off and on the ship. Members of the Cunard family, who had been on the lookout for the ship, had already been aboard for a tour and had gone ashore with their father to the family home on Brunswick Street, just a short distance from the ship, to get caught up on news.

Unfortunately for the welcoming committee, Halifax was the first to experience the time constraints inherent in a contract for the "regular delivery" of the mails by steamer. The committee had only just begun to formally congratulate the town's most distinguished native son when Captain Woodruff announced that the cargo, mails, and pilot were aboard, and the ship's bunkers were replenished with coal, and that the ship would sail within half an hour. Promptly at 9:00 a.m., the *Britannia* let go lines on the Cunard wharf and departed for Boston to a cannonade salute from the frigate *Winchester*. The ocean liner had been in Halifax just seven hours, half of them in

An 1849 portrait of Samuel Cunard
by Albert G. Hoit.

The Royal Engineer's lumberyard at
Greenbank, South End Halifax,
where Samuel Cunard worked as a
draftsman.

The house second from the right is 257 Brunswick Street, in Halifax—Samuel Cunard's residence.

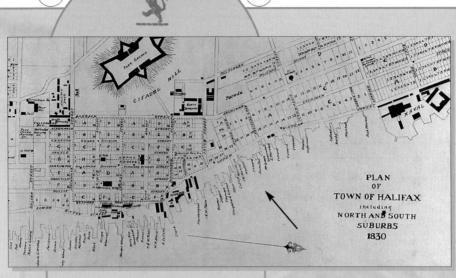

A detail of an 1830 plan of Halifax, showing the busy working waterfront, including the Cunard wharves (toward the right).

The Cunard warehouse on Upper Water Street, Halifax.

The Rawdon, Hants County, home that
Samuel Cunard built for his parents,
Abraham and Margaret.

A watercolour depicting the *Royal William* departing Pictou, Nova Scotia, for England on August 18, 1833.

The steam ferry *Sir Charles Ogle* arriving at the ferry dock in Halifax, circa 1833.

Oaklands, the residence of William
Cunard and Laura Charlotte
(Haliburton) Cunard, overlooking
the Northwest Arm in Halifax.

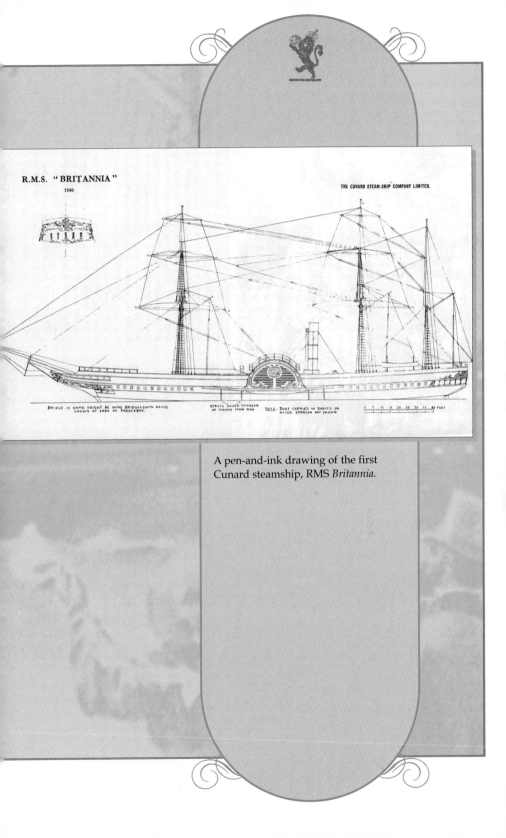

A pen-and-ink drawing of the first Cunard steamship, RMS *Britannia*.

A pen-and-ink drawing of Cunard mail
steamers in Halifax Harbour.

WRECK OF THE COLUMBIA STEAM-SHIP.

The Illustrated London News depiction of the July 1, 1843, loss of the Cunard Line steamship *Columbia* on Devil's Limb, Seal Island, in Nova Scotia.

'A view of Halifax Harbour c.1842, showing a steamer at the Cunard wharf and the steam ferry *Sir Charles Ogle* in foreground.

The Cunard coat of arms and motto.

The inaugural visit to Halifax, Nova Scotia, of the new Cunard Line flagship *Queen Mary 2*, on September 25, 2004.

CANADA 49

Sir Samuel Cunard

The Canada Post stamp commemorating Samuel Cunard, launched May 28, 2004.

A working model of the Cunard statue,
created by Halifax sculptor Peter Bustin,
to be erected on the Halifax waterfront.

darkness. It was the first example of the strict adherence to turn-around times in port that would be dictated initially by mail contracts, and today by the exacting standards imposed by cruise-ship schedules. Halifax's plans for a public reception would have to wait.

Bostonians were also eager to herald the *Britannia's* arrival, and went to extravagant lengths to honour Cunard. Although the ship arrived after dark—at 10:00 p.m. on July 18—there were great crowds of people waiting at the wharf to cheer as the ship docked. Three days later, "Cunard Festival Day" was celebrated in Boston— some said it was the biggest celebration in the Americas since the arrival of the *Mayflower*. An executive committee of thirteen prominent Bostonians, led by Robert G. Shaw, organized a two-thousand-person procession of guests from the Cunard wharf at East Boston to an elegantly decorated dinner pavilion at Maverick House.

Throughout the meal, many prominent individuals from among the invited guests took to the dais to extol the virtues of Cunard and his new line of steamships. Cunard responded with a brief speech, saying that even if he were prone to public speaking, he could never express his heartfelt gratitude for the reception he had been given. It was a momentous occasion, and it marked the beginning of a new age. Cunard's dreams had come true.

The *Britannia* returned to Halifax the first week in August 1840 from its triumphant visit to Boston. Once again, the Cunard wharves were the scene of uncommon animation during the six hours the ship laid over in its Halifax homeport. The local press had chastised the townspeople for failing to properly recognize Samuel Cunard during the few hours the ship had spent in Halifax two weeks earlier. The news about the Boston celebrations had made its way to Nova Scotia by then, and in an effort to placate its citizens, the *Acadian Recorder* newspaper published a rather defensive article on August 8, 1840:

We have heard our townsmen condemned by strangers for the apathy of their conduct towards the Honourable Mr. Cunard, while other cities have paid becoming homage to his enterprise

and talents; but, although the people of Halifax make no boisterous manifestations of their esteem for their illustrious and
worthy fellow townsman, yet their affection for him is more
deep-rooted and widespread than that of other communities
where everything has been tried to impress him with an idea of
his own merits and of their attachment to him.

As for Cunard, he was quite happy to be back home in the compara-
tive quiet of Halifax after the days of celebratory events in Boston,
which, although gratifying, had kept him before the public and away
from his business for longer than he wished. He had important family matters that now took his attention: his daughter Sarah Jane had
become engaged to Gilbert William Francklyn, a colonel in His
Majesty's Thirty-seventh Regiment. The wedding took place in
Halifax on September 1, 1840. As a wedding present Samuel gave his
daughter and new son-in-law a fine house, Emscote, built on the
slope of a hill overlooking the Northwest Arm. So began the connections between the Cunards and the Francklyns, who would later
assume roles in the management of the Halifax office of S. Cunard
and Company. Although the house is no longer standing, Emscote is
now a fashionable residential area off Francklyn Street in Halifax's
South End.

Cunard's three other new steamships were all put into transatlantic service in succession. The *Acadia* made its first voyage between
Liverpool and Boston in August, followed by the *Caledonia* in
September 1840. The fourth and last ship built, *Columbia*, arrived in
Halifax on its first transatlantic crossing in January 1841. All four settled quickly into regular service, and with some modifications,
Cunard's mail contract was carried out with great success. Crossings
were regularly advertised in the newspapers and gradually the passenger complement on the Cunard steamers increased, though on
many early crossings the crew outnumbered the passengers.

Charles Dickens, the celebrated English novelist and playwright,
was perhaps the first steamship travel writer. His first trip to

America, as a passenger aboard the *Britannia*, excited considerable public interest in ocean-liner travel when he later wrote about his experience in *American Notes*. Halifax was his first port of call in North America, where he, with his wife, Catherine, arrived aboard the *Britannia* on January 20, 1842, a day Dickens described as "uncommonly mild, the air bracing and healthful." He went on to say that he found "the whole aspect of the Town cheerful, thriving and industrious."

Soon after the ship was secured at the Cunard wharf, Dickens disembarked, and, in the company of the ship's doctor, walked a short distance to Upper Water Street and the European Hotel, where they enjoyed conversation while dining on oysters. He did not have long to enjoy his anonymity. Upon hearing of Dickens's arrival, Nova Scotia's leading statesman, Joseph Howe, accompanied by his wife, Susan Ann, went to the Cunard wharves to seek out and welcome the famous visitors. The ship and its passengers had endured a rough winter crossing of the North Atlantic. Catherine Dickens was under the weather; she was taken in tow by Susan Ann to the latter's home, while Joe Howe took Dickens to Nova Scotia's parliament chambers, where by chance it was the opening day of the legislature. Howe's guest was much impressed with the pomp and ceremony of the event, which he later wrote reminded him of a miniature British House of Parliament. As for Halifax, he wrote: "I carried away with me a most pleasing impression of the town and its inhabitants, and have preserved it to this hour."

After an eventful day in Halifax, the *Britannia* and the Dickenses continued to Boston. Samuel Cunard accompanied them. Captain John Hewitt was in command of the ship. The voyage from Liverpool had been particularly rough, but the voyage had been completed without incident. The relieved passengers expressed their gratitude by subscribing three hundred dollars for a piece of silver plate for Captain Hewitt. Charles Dickens acted as secretary and treasurer for the presentation of this testimonial gift; his first public appearance in the United States was at the Tremont Theatre in Boston to honour

Captain Hewitt and present him with the plate as a public token of his gratitude for bringing he and his fellow passengers safely to America.

This type of event was repeated many times with Cunard captains, particularly in the early years of steam. On this occasion, the credit due the *Britannia* was given publicly, but it was by the unrecorded repetition of such feats, year after year, that the Cunard Line attained its well-known reputation of safety and seamanship.

The impact Cunard and his first mail ships had on intercontinental trade and commerce cannot be overstated. During the decade of the 1840s, following the advent of the Cunard service, foreign trade in Boston more than doubled. By 1850, import duties collected in Boston had increased to five million dollars annually—sometimes as high as a hundred thousand dollars on a single cargo arriving aboard a Cunard steamer.

The best example of the importance of the new Cunard steam service to Boston was an event that occurred in the winter of 1844. By then Boston, an ice-free port, had become quite accustomed to and reliant upon the regular service afforded to it as the North American terminus of the Cunard Line. That winter, however, was particularly harsh. February 1 found the *Britannia* at its dock in East Boston, ready to depart for Liverpool in accordance with its schedule. Due to extreme cold, however, the harbour froze, trapping the *Britannia* at its berth. Its schedule, long since held by Boston merchants to be infallible, was in jeopardy. They immediately struck a committee that raised fifteen hundred dollars, enough to pay the cost of cutting a channel seven miles long out of the harbour and to the open sea. The *Britannia* would by this means escape winter's icy grip in Boston, from whence it departed just two days behind schedule.

Cunard's new steamship service quickly established a spirit of goodwill between New England and Britain, arising out of the direct contact and tremendous expansion in trade between the Old and New worlds. This new feeling of friendship also extended to the United States and Canada. In 1844 the American Congress passed an act authorizing the transmission, duty free, of goods from Europe, via Boston, to Canada. This came about in part through Cunard's representations in Washington and would lead to the Reciprocity Treaty of 1854. It, and the role Cunard played in it, helped establish a mutual confidence between the two countries that has remained ever since as a model of international friendliness and cooperation.

Cunard, however, was not without his detractors in the United States. The early success of his line and the inroads it quickly made in commerce did not go unnoticed by American businessmen and their lobbyists in Washington. Congress was initially taken aback by the first voyage of the *Britannia* and the threat that steam now posed to sail, heretofore the backbone and pride of the American merchant marine. Some politicians argued that Britain had chosen Samuel Cunard as its instrument and, through him, had issued America a challenge that it could ill afford to ignore. Debate reached the point of fear-mongering, as evidenced by the words addressed to Congress by Senator Bayard of Delaware: "The treasury of Britain is to be poured into the lap of this man Cunard for the sole purpose of destroying the interests of our beloved country and for building up a merchant marine at the expense of the commerce and future prosperity of America. Therefore, gentlemen, I for one, shall count no cost in countervailing such a despicable action by Britain."

When one Senator suggested the US might consider protectionism as a means of combating the British supremacy of the Atlantic brought about by steam, the outspoken senator from Delaware was quick to respond, saying: "That type of protection I submit means only one thing—speed! Speed against which these British can never hope to compete. Speed of a magnitude such as the government of Britain and its chosen instrument, this man Cunard, never visualized or could ever hope to achieve against America!"

Not even the President of the United States, James K. Polk, was immune from such rhetoric. When in 1845 he addressed Congress on the subject, Polk adopted a similar line when he proclaimed: "When the treasury of some other nation is poured into the lap of one chosen individual for the sole purpose of destroying America, I say that we must act, and act now!"

A few years later Congress did act. A large subsidy was provided to Edward Knight Collins, a New York merchant and highly success-ful shipowner who also believed the future lay in steam. He and the Collins Line would briefly challenge Cunard for the supremacy of the North Atlantic. The Collins ships were well built and far superi-or to Cunard liners in finishings and amenities. However, in an effort to acquire with speed what the Cunard Line had accomplished with safety and reliability, the Collins liners met with one disaster after the other.

The SS *Atlantic* and the SS *Pacific* were launched for the Collins Line February 1, 1849, and after a year of extensive and elaborate fit-ting out, were brought into service in competition with Cunard in 1850. The new Collins ships were much larger, more powerful, and considerably more opulent than the conservative *Britannia* and other Cunard ships, and Collins enjoyed success at Cunard's expense on the North Atlantic for a few years until calamity beset the company. In September 1854 the Collins liner *Artic* collided in dense fog with the French steamship *Vesta* and sank. Many of the 322 lost were wealthy American passengers, among them Collins's own wife, son, and daughter. The loss of the *Artic* was a horrific blow to the compa-ny and its founder. As if this wasn't enough, not much more than a year later the Collins steamship *Pacific* departed Liverpool for a scheduled crossing of the Atlantic in January 1854–55 with 114 crew and 45 passengers. The *Pacific* disappeared without a trace, together with all aboard. Quite apart from the negative publicity arising out of the company's dismal safety record, the Collins Line incurred crip-pling expense in maintaining machinery. Their steamers were run hard. The cost proved ruinous.

In a last attempt to recover from losses of both the *Artic* and the *Pacific*, in 1857 Collins built his final steamship, the *Adriatic*, at the extraordinary cost of 1.2 million dollars. But it was too late; the com-pany's financial condition was beyond recovery. The Collins plight was summed up by Charles MacIver in a letter to Samuel Cunard: "The Collins people are pretty much in the situation of finding that breaking our windows with sovereigns, though very fine fun, is too costly to keep on."

Cunard gained and kept control of the North Atlantic steamship monopoly through a dedication to reliability and safety above all else.

CHAPTER 9

SAFETY AND SEAMANSHIP

The North Atlantic is the harshest ocean in the world. There climate conditions conspire to produce the "perfect storms" into which countless ships and crews have vanished without a trace. Edward Knight Collins found this to be so in his failed attempt to sweep Cunard from the Atlantic.

Canada's Maritime Provinces face east toward England, some three thousand miles across the storm-tossed waters. Nova Scotia is almost an island, joined to the mainland only by a narrow isthmus and surrounded by some of the most challenging waters on earth. To the north is the Gulf of St. Lawrence, named after the mighty inland waterway providing access to Canada's Great Lakes and the American interior. Prince Edward Island, the "Garden of the Gulf," is separated from Nova Scotia by the warm, shallow waters of Northumberland Strait. Ships travelling east from there, depending on their size, may choose to go around Cape Breton Island, the northernmost part of Nova Scotia, and into the Cabot Strait, the ninety-mile breadth of water that separates Nova Scotia from Newfoundland, or to transit the Strait of Canso and the Canso canal in the causeway that has joined mainland Nova Scotia to Cape Breton Island since 1955.

To the east, of course, are the deep blue waters of the North Atlantic. Nova Scotia is girdled on the south by the waters of the Gulf of Maine and on the west by the Bay of Fundy, which daily produces the world's highest tides. The geography of this province is such that no one lives more than forty miles from water. Nova Scotia's people and economy have been shaped by the sea surrounding them. During the twentieth century and to this day, Nova Scotia has been marketed to tourists as "Canada's Ocean Playground." In the nineteenth century, however, it was anything but. Nova Scotia, the other Maritime Provinces, and Newfoundland were all workplaces, and for a time, Nova Scotia was the fourth-largest producer of ships in the world. Its shorelines were dotted with shipyards that launched countless vessels renowned internationally for their quality and workmanship.

To the mariner who approaches from the east, the coast of Nova Scotia can be intimidating and dangerous. With the exception of the Cape Breton Highlands in the extreme north, Nova Scotia has a very low topography and is an indistinct landmass from even very close offshore. Even with charts and other aids to navigation, the modern sailor is hard-pressed to pick out landmarks on shore to confirm position or guide the ship to a safe harbour. The mere sighting of land can give small comfort. The east and south coasts of Nova Scotia are strewn with islands and jagged outcrops of rock that can quickly impale the hull of the unwary and are often hidden from view by tides and stormy seas. Constant vigilance is required even in the best of conditions.

Samuel Cunard was one of those most involved in wooden ship construction before he turned his attention to steam, and he was also a sailor who was very much at home at sea. While amassing his large fleet of ships and building up his vast shipping empire, Cunard spent a great deal of time aboard his vessels. In this way he gained valuable experience about the perils and pitfalls that beset captain and crew looking to make port in Nova Scotia.

From his earliest childhood days he had been acutely aware of the hazards of navigating Nova Scotia's dark coast. Cunard was just ten years old when the British frigate *La Tribune* floundered and sank off

Thrum Cap Shoals, near the entrance to Halifax Harbour. The ago-
nizing cries from those aboard the ship could be heard from shore.
Despite best efforts to rescue the hapless passengers and crew, by
dawn the next day some 240 men, women, and children had perished. This tragedy had a profound impact on Samuel Cunard and
offers some explanation for his intense interest in lighthouses, of
which there were only a handful in Nova Scotia in 1816, the year he
was made a lighthouse commissioner by then-lieutenant-governor,
John Coape Sherbrooke.

He and the other two commissioners were given a broad mandate
"to take charge of and superintend the several lighthouses now erected or which may hereafter be erected on the coasts of this province."
It was a post that Cunard would retain for more than forty years,
during which time he played a direct role in the building of many
new lighthouses. Two lightstations in particular serve to illustrate
Cunard's preoccupation with coastal navigation and "safety and seamanship," which became hallmarks of the Cunard Line.

The first was located on the so-called Graveyard of the Gulf. St.
Paul Island is a three-mile-long, wind-swept island lying in the
Cabot Strait about fifteen miles off Cape North, Cape Breton, and
forty-five miles southwest of Cape Ray on the southwest coast of
Newfoundland. Apart from Trinity Cove on the west and Atlantic
Cove on the east side, both of which offer minimal protection from
swells and weather, there are few places to set foot on this island in
safety. Even in the best of summer conditions, to get ashore in the
modest anchorage provided by Atlantic Cove, one must first find a
place to land a tender and then scale a thirty-foot cliff to access the
rough ground of the island proper.

Lying directly in the path of ships bound for or leaving the Gulf of
St. Lawrence, St. Paul Island has long been a principal hazard on a
very busy thoroughfare. With heavy seas, dense fog, and treacherous
currents prevalent in this area, the island deserves its nickname; it is
the final resting place of thousands of unknown men, women, and
children who have been shipwrecked on its shores. Cunard knew the

area and the island quite well as a result of his frequent passage aboard his own ships, as they travelled to Newfoundland and Prince Edward Island.

The need for a lighthouse there was made painfully clear to him when he lost his younger brother William, an up-and-coming Halifax merchant, in the wreck of the *Wyton*. On November 23, 1823, William was a passenger aboard the British ship when it was wrecked off Cape North.

In 1838, after years of government waffling, the Nova Scotia Lighthouse Commissioners were finally authorized to proceed with the construction of two lighthouses—the northeast and southwest lights—on St. Paul Island. Samuel Cunard took on the tasks of determining the location of both lights and the lifesaving station, and of organizing staffing. Through his office and connections in Pictou, Cunard had made the acquaintance of John Campbell, a Scottish immigrant. Campbell was placed in charge of both lights and the lightstation, assuming the position of governor of St. Paul Island. Under his direction the northeast light cast its first beacon into the Atlantic in December 1839; the southwest light was lit in June 1840.

John Campbell performed his duties faithfully for almost twenty years, during which the number and frequency of shipwrecks was substantially reduced. There were still tragedies, but many crews of ships that fetched up on St. Paul Island's unforgiving shores were rescued and given shelter by the lightkeepers; in the years before the establishment of the lights, those who survived shipwrecks and somehow managed to make it ashore had died of exposure and starvation.

At the opposite end of Nova Scotia lies another island, which, until the establishment of a lighthouse there, also served as a graveyard for hundreds of vessels.

Seal Island was named in 1604 by European explorer Samuel de Champlain for the large number of seals basking on its shores. Approximately twenty miles from Clarke's Harbour on the southwest coast of Nova Scotia, it is located at the elbow of the Bay of

Fundy, where the deep, open waters of the Atlantic converge upon the wide mouth of the bay—a juncture where frequent fog, tricky ocean currents, and high tides have conspired to bring the best of ships and sailors to grief on the island's rocky ledges.

Seal Island is about the same size and shape as St. Paul Island, but lacks its elevation. Its hard-packed sand beaches look inviting but disguise the harsh reality that, until lifesaving stations were established in 1823 by the Hichens and Crowell families, many of those who managed to get ashore from ships fetched up on the rock ledges that encircle the island died a lingering death due to exposure and starvation during the winter months when Seal Island was inaccessible. For years, spring proved to be a sombre time for fishermen from the mainland who, when winter abated, would visit the island to bury the bodies of those washed ashore, or others who had died from cold and starvation on the uninhabited island.

Once settled, the Hichenses and Crowells began a long association with Seal Island that spanned generations. Through their humanitarian efforts, it could be said that no one cast upon the island's shores would die from lack of food and cover. This would provide great comfort to Samuel Cunard some years later when his fledgling transatlantic steamship company would survive one of its only shipwrecks.

A few years after moving onto the island, the Crowells petitioned Lieutenant-Governor James Kempt first for a wharf and then for a lighthouse. In 1827 Kempt visited the island and saw firsthand the need for a light. More petitions followed. Finally, with the encouragement of Cunard, who had lived through William's death and saw a clear need for a light to protect his own ships, regularly plying those waters, the Nova Scotia House of Assembly voted for a grant of five hundred pounds towards the costs of construction. New Brunswick agreed to contribute the remaining half of the cost.

Work got underway in 1830 at the south end of the island, and on November 28, 1831, the Seal Island lighthouse went into operation. It is a sixty-seven-foot-high wooden octagonal structure that operates to this day. The Seal Island lighthouse tower is the oldest timber-frame lighthouse in Nova Scotia, and one of only two of such structures in Canada. Unfortunately, the lighthouse would not prevent the loss of one of Cunard's brand new steamships when in 1843 the Royal Mail steamer *Columbia* wrecked on the reef appropriately known as Devil's Limb, within sight of the Seal Island Lighthouse.

The *Columbia* was one of the four steamships with which Cunard began the transatlantic mail service in 1840. The four steamships' tight schedule between Liverpool, Halifax, and Boston had been maintained without any major incident through fair and foul weather until 1843.

On Saturday, July 2, 1843, the *Columbia* was en route from Boston to Halifax when it grounded in thick fog upon Devil's Limb. It was carrying eighty-five passengers and seventy-three crew, under the command of Captain Shannon. Although travelling at reduced speed under steam, its forward motion was enough to carry it high up on the reef, elevate its bow, and rest it upon a pivot.

Immediately upon striking at 10:00 a.m., in calm seas, Captain Shannon ordered alarm guns fired, not knowing that Seal Island was less than two miles distant, hidden as it was in the fog. To his relief and, undoubtedly, that of both passengers and crew, the ship's alarm guns and bell were answered from shore and shortly afterwards they were joined by rescue boats full of members of both the Crowell and Hichens families. They arranged to take the women and some men ashore. Most of the men remained aboard overnight to assist in efforts to extricate the ship from the deadly grip of Devil's Limb. Their best efforts proved useless. With the bow out of the water, weight was concentrated midships; the beautiful liner, one of the four finest vessels afloat, became hogged—broken in the middle—and eventually went to pieces on the shoal.

Once their situation was known, captain and crew concentrated all efforts in removing the remaining passengers to safety ashore. Soon all souls were in the care of the Crowells and Hichenses, severely taxing their modest accommodations on Seal Island.

Shortly after the *Columbia* struck, the sailing ship *Acadian*, out of Boston, arrived on the scene. It had almost been drawn to the same fate by the very tides that swept the *Columbia* off course. It took the *Columbia's* third mate to Halifax where they arrived late on July 4 to the Cunard wharves and an anxious Samuel Cunard. Until now, no one had heard of the fate of the *Columbia*, which was uncharacteristically overdue for its scheduled arrival in Halifax. Quite apart from concern for passengers and crew, the contract with the British Admiralty contained severe penalties for late delivery of the mails.

Concerned over the plight of his ship, but relieved that all passengers and crew were safe, Cunard took immediate action to provision his relief steamer, the *Margaret*, in which he promptly set off to meet passengers and crew from the ill-fated mail steamer. The *Margaret* steamed into sight at Seal Island on July 6, much to the delight and relief of all on the island. During the next two days, Cunard personally oversaw the evacuation of all passengers and crew to the *Margaret*. It, together with mail and anything salvageable from the *Columbia* set off for Halifax, where it arrived on July 8. The following day, the *Margaret*, under command of Captain Shannon, departed for Liverpool, to the delight and cheers of the large crowd gathered at the Cunard wharves to see it off.

Cunard's immediate response to the *Columbia* disaster was typical of the man. There was no hesitation on his part—attending in person to the immediate rescue of passengers and crew of the ill-fated liner was simply the right thing to do. His method was straightforward and simple—observation and careful assessment followed by action.

Cunard was relieved to see a happy conclusion to what could have been a tragic affair on board the *Columbia*. Ships could always be replaced, as was the *Columbia* with the larger *Cambria* in 1845. He knew too well that what could not be so easily replaced were passengers and crew, and the reputation of a company founded on the principles of safety and seamanship. True, in the years to come the Cunard Line would lose many ships to weather and collision at sea;

the North Atlantic is, after all, a tempestuous workplace that has claimed countless ships and their occupants. To this very day, however, the Cunard Line can still boast that it has never lost a single passenger at sea due to negligence—a record that stands unchallenged by the company's many competitors, past and present.

Cunard remained a lighthouse commissioner throughout his career, and when in the mid-nineteenth century the Lighthouse Commission was disbanded and control of those structures turned over to the Department of Public Works, Cunard wrote strongly on the subject, advocating that the lighthouse commissioners be kept in place and not dissolved in favour of a board of works, which "will have plenty of duty on shore." (Given the current state of lighthouses in Nova Scotia, Cunard's advice may have had merit.)

One might well ask what allows the Cunard Line to stand alone with its enviable record of safety at sea. Some would suggest that the answer lies in Cunard luck, and certainly there is often an element of luck that makes the difference between a sad or happy ending to any disaster at sea. (The *Columbia*, had it struck bottom during a gale in mid-February, might indeed have produced a tragic ending to what was otherwise a happy story.) Another part of the answer lies in Cunard employees—their character, business acumen, and, more importantly, their humanitarianism. For the Cunard Line, this inherent strength began with the founder, Samuel Cunard, and continued with those he gathered about him, beginning with his original partners, their successors, and ultimately the captains and crews of Cunard ships. Through them these fundamental strengths have been demonstrated time and time again.

Seamanship and experience often separate Cunarders from competitors. Many of those who work with Cunard serve with the company for twenty-five years or more. It is not uncommon for children to follow parents and grandparents onto Cunard ships, to work for their entire careers.

Another facet of the Cunard tradition of safety that was established very early on is the element of ruggedness of both the crews and the vessels themselves. The first quartet of Cunard mail steamers was built plain but strong at the insistence of Cunard, and despite Edward Knight Collins's and other competitors' larger, faster, and more opulent ships, Cunard—ever conservative and cautious—gained an enviable and unsurpassed reputation for safe and dependable delivery of mails and passengers alike.

After 166 years of uninterrupted service (except during wartime), the Cunard Line is still a model of both safety and seamanship, thanks to the principles and policies set forth by Samuel Cunard.

CHAPTER 10

THE BUSINESS IN CRISIS

Despite Cunard's success in introducing steam to the Atlantic, his mail contract with the British Admiralty was producing lower-than-expected profits in the spring of 1842. This had been apparent to Cunard since the year before, when he had written expressing his concerns to his partner David MacIver in Liverpool. MacIver's response was one of encouragement, suggesting that 1841 had been an experimental year and that they would soon find profit.

MacIver's positive spin on the business was not enough, however, to assuage Cunard's creditors. In September Cunard arranged to borrow a large sum from the British and North American Royal Mail Steam Packet Company. In addition, he mortgaged his 110 original shares and all rights in the steamship company and in five steam vessels registered in Glasgow. Profits and dividends on shares of stock and commissions due to Cunard or to his son Edward, as the company's agent in North America, were to be used to pay interest on the loan and pay for the stock subscription. Samuel was allowed five percent on the gross earnings of the ships, which amounted to between eight and ten thousand pounds annually. This was a considerable sum, but it was not available to Cunard — instead, it was to be placed to his credit until the steamship shares were fully paid, at which time his creditors would receive any profits made.

Personal finances were therefore very much on Cunard's mind in the spring of 1842. He was over-extended and financially vulnerable for the first time in his life. Cunard was considered by many to be one of the wealthiest men in Nova Scotia, and at the top of his game, but he knew otherwise. Over the next few months he would have to call upon all his skills and resources to avoid the spectres of failure and defeat.

For three years Cunard had been on a mercantile roller-coaster ride. Although he had been preparing himself for some time to enter the North Atlantic steamship arena, the tender call by the British Admiralty in late 1838 was not at a time of his choosing. Given the choice, he would probably have waited a bit longer before embarking on the greatest challenge of his life. His stunning successes in arranging the shipbuilding contract with Robert Napier, securing the postal contract from the Admiralty, and bringing about the incorporation of the British and North American Royal Mail Steam Packet Company were not without repercussions for Cunard, and they were financial in nature.

There were signs of impending troubles back in 1838; Cunard had devoted so much of his time to the creation and launch of the new steamship line that something had to suffer. Financial difficulties first appeared in the different branches of the Cunard business empire in the Maritimes. These unwelcome developments were exacerbated by the significant borrowings by Cunard for his transatlantic steamships. All gave rise to Cunard's financial crisis of 1842.

Cunard had spent twenty-two thousand pounds on about 162,000 acres of land in PEI in 1838, financed by bankers in London, England; he was asset rich but cash poor. Compounding his troubles was his brother Joseph, who was proving to be quite his opposite as a businessman in Miramichi.

He had built up Joseph Cunard and Company enormously, with timber berths scattered over a large area, between the Jacquet River on the Bay of Chaleur and the Kouchibouguac River in Kent County. In Chatham, Joseph had built wharves, offices, and a new steam sawmill, and had shortly thereafter created similar operations in neighbouring Gloucester counties. He soon dominated business in Bathurst, where he acquired houses, stores, and wharves, to accommodate timber taken from his land on the Nepisiguit River. When the Bathurst timber trade suffered a depression in 1837, Joseph formed shipbuilding operations there.

His shipbuilding activities were extensive; by 1839 he had two shipyards of his own in Chatham, and soon had yards in Richibucto and Kouchibouguac. Making work and spawning new businesses, often without any regard for the bottom line, were Joseph's specialties. He met with much success, but when Henry, his younger brother and partner, decided to leave the firm in 1841, the business was jeopardized — Henry was undoubtedly a moderating influence on his brother. This came at a time when Samuel had just begun his mails contract, and so had less time to devote to the Miramichi operation as well.

By the spring of 1842, word around Chatham was that their local champion, Joseph Cunard, was in trouble. In a letter dated March 26, 1842, Michael Samuel, a prominent Chatham businessman, wrote to Messrs. Moses, Son and Davis:

> I assure you all is gloom here [Chatham] waiting the arrival of the March mail and all are anxious respecting the Cunards. I am afraid it is up with them. I need not tell you I am sorry as I shall be a looser to the amount of 8,000–10,000 pounds...this will blast all my prospects for the future.

Almost ten years earlier, unbeknownst to Cunard, Joseph Howe had expressed his private concern over the future of the Cunard enterprise in the Miramichi. In a letter written to his wife on May 11, 1834, Howe remarked that: "The Cunards are making a great dash here [Miramichi] but all I can see of them confirms my opinion of the ultimate smash of the whole concern."

There was substance to Howe's fears. Within a few days of Michael Samuel's letter, Joseph Cunard and Company and S. Cunard and Company, a substantial creditor of Joseph's business, together with Joseph, Edward, and Samuel Cunard, themselves came to an agreement with the many creditors of the Chatham firm. The agreement forbade the Cunards from entering upon any new business and allowed them three years to sell off property to meet liabilities. Fortunately Joseph Cunard and Company held the titles to vast tracts of land, some of which were sold off over time, enabling Joseph to avoid total financial embarrassment for the moment. For his brother Samuel, however, money problems were about to take a turn for the worst.

Cunard, who had to this point been using all his diplomacy and tact to placate his London creditors, finally experienced the inevitable when the Liverpool banking firm of Leyland and Bullen took out a writ of attachment against him for two thousand pounds. Knowing that service of the writ might precipitate a chain reaction with other creditors and potentially interrupt his mail service, Cunard took the extreme measure of going underground.

Duncan Gibb, a friend and Liverpool agent for the firm of Pollok, Gilmour and Company, immediately provided refuge for Samuel in a cottage on the Mersey River near Liverpool. The next day Cunard was brought down to the river by Gibb's boatman shortly before one of the Cunard steamers, bound for Halifax, slipped its mooring. A few of Cunard's creditors, armed with writs of their own, and suspecting that he might try to leave the country, were aboard until the last minute, eventually leaving, exasperated, on boats. Shortly after getting underway, and before the creditors had made it back to shore, the steamer slackened speed, allowing Cunard's boat to run alongside. Samuel boarded—no doubt to his great relief, and to the ultimate gain of the Cunard Line.

Cunard's total indebtedness at this time was 130,000 pounds. Although his assets far exceeded his liabilities, he had a definite cash flow problem. He used his time during the Atlantic crossing to plan his strategy for avoiding insolvency, and when he arrived back in Halifax he immediately began to put his financial house in order. He began with the liquidation of some of his many assets—lands in Prince Edward Island sold at a profit. The farm in Rawdon bought by Samuel years ago for his parents was sold to the caretaker, Thomas Meehan (and remains in the Meehan family to this day).

Samuel then turned to his friends and family for help. The Cunard wharves, warehouses, and premises on Upper Water Street in Halifax were mortgaged for nine thousand pounds to Stephen Wastie DeBlois, a merchant and auctioneer friend. Then the Duffuses were able to turn the tables and help Cunard in his time of need. Samuel's brother-in-law, John Duffus, used his considerable influence with the Bank of Nova Scotia and the Bank of British North America to extricate Cunard from his financial predicament. An account of the role played by the Bank of Nova Scotia in the refinancing of the Cunard business provides an opportunity to consider the importance of the relationship of Samuel Cunard, S. Cunard and Company, and the fledgling Bank of Nova Scotia.

Back in 1825, when Cunard was an original partner of the private Halifax Banking Company, the bank began to attract a fair number of detractors—those who felt that the bank had become a monopoly, bringing large profits into the hands of a few wealthy merchant-directors, five of whom were members of the Upper Council of the Province of Nova Scotia—the Council of Twelve to which Cunard had been appointed in 1830. After many petitions and debates, a public bank was established to counter the Halifax Banking Company's monopoly—the Bank of Nova Scotia was born.

One of the new bank's most important clients was the General Mining Association, and when Cunard—still a director of the Halifax Banking Company—became agent for the GMA, the Bank of Nova Scotia was certain that they would lose their lucrative client—but Cunard surprised them.

On July 20, 1834, an incredulous bank President William Lawson wrote the bank's London agent, Henry Bliss: "Mr. Cunard, as Agent of the General Mining Association continues to transact the company's business at the Bank of Nova Scotia!" That bank continued to deal with the GMA for years to come.

Cunard's surprising support of the Bank of Nova Scotia probably had a lot to do with the bank's response to Cunard's financial distress a few years later. Cunard approached them for financial assistance through John Duffus, then a dry goods merchant in Halifax and a customer of the bank. Cunard sought a loan that was, by that time's banking standards, staggering: forty-five thousand pounds. He believed that amount, paired with the extension of some debts, would see him through the worst of his troubles. The amount he requested was approximately one third of the entire paid-up capital of the bank and more than double the authorized limit for advances! A special meeting of the bank board was convened in the Hollis Street head office on April 5, 1842, "for consideration of the proposition made to the Bank by Messrs. S. Cunard and Company, the embarrassed state of whose affairs had on several previous days received the attention of the board."

After much discussion and deliberation, the bank president, Hon. M. B. Almon, was authorized to address a letter to the manager of the Bank of British North America "to express the willingness of the Bank of Nova Scotia to meet that bank on equal terms in rendering the requisite assistance to the firm in question." A committee composed of John Duffus and four Bank of Nova Scotia directors was appointed to act as trustees for the property of Samuel, Edward, and Joseph Cunard under the proposed arrangement. The trustees of Cunard's English creditors, which included the Bank of Liverpool, North and South Wales Bank, and Prescott's Bank, were three prominent London businessmen.

With the loan approved, Cunard pledged virtually all of his worldly goods, including his furniture, to the bank. He also lost his mobility—the man who had just revolutionized transatlantic travel was forbidden to leave his place of business without permission from the trustees, possibly because they had heard about Cunard's underground escape from Liverpool, and possibly because of the sheer magnitude of Cunard's debt. To compensate, Cunard's son Edward, accompanied by his cousin Robert Morrow, travelled back and forth to England as envoys for the firm while Cunard devoted his attention to company business at home.

Almost immediately after he settled into his new work mode and begun to pay down his accumulated debt was Cunard confronted with more financial strife, brought on by Joseph. Joseph had managed to overcome his financial difficulties in 1842, and continued to run Joseph Cunard and Company in Miramichi. However, by the mid-1840s it was clear that he had in fact run the company into the ground. Joseph's business practices remained unchanged and his company had now reached an irreversible state of indebtedness. In an effort to separate their business from Joseph's, Samuel and Edward advertised that the partnership between Joseph Cunard and Company and S. Cunard and Company would be dissolved on December 31, 1845. It was none too soon. Within two years the inevitable occurred: In November 1847, unable to meet its financial obligations, Joseph Cunard declared his company bankrupt.

It was left to Samuel Cunard to bear the great burden of his brother's failure. He set about the task of arranging to pay all the creditors of Joseph Cunard and Company, although legally he was not obliged to do so. Fortunately for Samuel, during the previous few years profits from the steamship company had increased and had methodically been applied towards the loan from the Nova Scotia trustees. On April 1, 1846, a formal deed was signed reconveying the steamship stock—and thus its profits—that Samuel and his son Edward had pledged as part of the security for the loan.

The relief within his steamship company is evident in a letter sent to Samuel Cunard from his Liverpool partner, George Burns, dated March 14, 1846:

> My Dear Friend...it is with sincere pleasure I enclose for your perusal the drafts of two deeds for discharging the money matters between you and the Company. I congratulate you on the

happy termination of these affairs, which were at one time somewhat intricate, and hope you and your son will long be spared to enjoy the fruits of your exertions.

Cunard continued to exert himself, and with a tenacity and single-mindedness of purpose that spoke to his Quaker heritage, he managed to raise sufficient capital to pay off the Bank of Nova Scotia and Halifax Banking Company indebtedness by December 1850. It took much longer and he never lived to see it, but the debts of Joseph Cunard and Company to Chatham were paid off by 1871. No one could ever question Samuel Cunard's integrity.

Despite what must have been a constant preoccupation during the 1840s with the financial health of his struggling business empire, Cunard still found time to spend with his family in Halifax. There were moments of both sadness and pleasure. On April 21, 1844, his brother John, who had spent most of his life at sea as the captain of various family vessels, died in Halifax at the age of forty-four. Though never married, in his will John left a lot and premises at Upper Water Street in Halifax, plus a modest sum of money, to Emily Carritt, a teller at the Bank of British North America. He was buried in the Old Dutch Churchyard, not far from the place of his birth on Brunswick Street.

There were also many celebrations in the family. St. George's Round Church in Halifax was the scene of three Cunard weddings during Cunard's financial crisis, two less than a year apart. On October 19, 1843, Samuel's daughter Margaret Ann, named after her paternal grandmother, married William Leigh Mellish, a captain in the Rifle Brigade from Norfolk, England. On September 7, 1844, her younger sister Anne Elizabeth was married to another military man, Ralph Shuttleworth Allen, a lieutenant in the Royal Artillery from Bathampton, England. A few years later, on October 21, 1850, as Cunard was completing his final payments to the Bank of Nova Scotia, another daughter, Isabella, married Henry Holden of Nuttall Temple, England.

With most of his time in the 1840s being spent at home in Halifax, Samuel Cunard was present to experience the growth of his family during their adolescent years. In a sense, for his younger children, their famous father's financial crisis had a silver lining, bringing the family together as it did during these formative years. That was about to change. The bank loan now paid, Cunard was again free to travel, and almost immediately he resumed his visits to England, returning to a more active role in the management of the steamship company. He had just re-established a work schedule that saw him travelling back and forth between Liverpool, Halifax, Boston, and New York when his brother Edward died suddenly at Halifax in 1851. Edward was married to Margaret Jane Yeomans, daughter of Henry Yeomans, a Halifax insurance broker. He had not played any significant role in S. Cunard and Company in the years prior to his death; he was only involved with the company through his real estate holdings.

By this time the steamship company had become well established in the transatlantic service, and was finally making a good amount of profit. The original quartet of steamers had been joined by progressively larger and faster steamships—the *Hibernia*, the *Cambria*, the *America*, the *Niagara*, the *Europa*, the *Canada*, the *Asia*, and the *Africa* all became part of the Cunard fleet. Each would attain fame during their years of service on the North Atlantic.

As the fleet and the company expanded, it became clear to Cunard that he would have to devote most of his time to the steamship company. Since the principals and shareholders of the British and North American Royal Mail Steam Packet Company were located in and about the port of Liverpool, it was evident that Cunard would have to move to England.

By this time New York had taken over from Boston as the main terminus in America for the Cunard Line, and Samuel had arranged for his son Edward to move to New York, where he managed the interests of the company in the United States. Edward was continuing to prove to be a capable businessman. On May 17, 1849, he had married Mary Bache McEvers, daughter of Bache McEvers, a New York merchant. Edward and Mary built a large mansion at Grymes Hill, a thirty-eight-acre estate on Staten Island. The house had a commanding view of New York's harbour, Manhattan, and the Atlantic Ocean. From there Edward could watch the ships of the Cunard Line arrive from and depart for England. The house served in the late nineteenth century as one of the social centres for the Staten Island elite, and stands today as Cunard Hall, part of Wagner College on Staten Island.

With the American aspect of his company in place, Cunard put his younger son William in charge of the Halifax firm, aided by Samuel's nephew James Bain Morrow. Twenty-five in 1850, William had a head for business, though he did not have the same energy or initiative that drove his father. Initially William continued to live at home at 257 Brunswick Street in Halifax, but in 1851 he married Laura Charlotte Haliburton, daughter of Judge Thomas Chandler Haliburton, and they built a splendid house, Oaklands, overlooking Halifax's Northwest Arm. The gatehouse of the original estate still exists and can be seen behind the stone pillars that lead into the property at the corner of Robie Street and Oakland Road in Halifax. This is one of the few remaining vestiges of the Cunard family in Halifax.

Samuel Cunard maintained the original family home in Halifax, but by the mid-1850s he had taken up residence in London, England, with his youngest daughter, Elizabeth, and by 1858 was signing contracts that stated his English residence as his permanent address.

Cunard was by no means ready to rest on his laurels at this time. After years of relative peace, war now offered him yet further opportunity and recognition beyond his greatest expectations.

CHAPTER 11

WAR AND ARISTOCRACY

The underlying strength of Cunard's steamship line—his partnership with Napier, Burns, and MacIver—was never more effectively demonstrated than during the last half of the 1840s, when Cunard was consumed with keeping his financial house afloat. During this time the three Scottish principals oversaw the crucial formative years of the fledgling transatlantic steamship service. Cunard contributed to management of the Cunard Line only from a distance and with the aid of his son Edward.

By 1850 the Cunard fleet numbered twelve steamships, all engined by Robert Napier; the *Asia* and the *Africa*, both launched in 1850, were twice the tonnage of the first flagship, the *Britannia*, reflecting the rapid changes already occurring in the industry. This number more than doubled before the end of the decade. Change was not restricted to size alone, however; by 1860, the paddlewheel gave way to screw propulsion, and steel hulls replaced wood. From the start Cunard adopted a very conservative approach to change, preferring to let the competition experiment with new innovations, and only adopting them once they were proven to be successful. Although he and his partners sometimes disagreed on the practicality of new concepts in engineering and design, Cunard's consistently conservative approach meant that each new Cunard ship was an improvement on the last, without any disastrous attempts at innovations.

There were other changes, quite apart from technology and engineering, that were impacting the transatlantic service. What had begun just a few years previously as the transatlantic Royal Mail Steam Packet Company was already in transition. Regular delivery of the English mails to the colonies, which had lead to the call for tenders by the British Admiralty, was now being overshadowed by socio-economic development. In Europe the Industrial Revolution was creating its own form of unemployment—craftspeople were becoming destitute while increased population and crop failures were bringing whole agricultural communities to the verge of starvation. In sharp contrast, America was rapidly expanding westward, faster than pioneers were born to fill the vast new land. The lure of a new life in America gave rise to a mass movement of emigrants from Europe. The Atlantic Ocean separated them from their new homeland.

This emigration totally changed the commerce of ocean travel and the face of America, and during the 1850s alone almost three million people emigrated from the Old to the New World. This movement, which was to become the greatest migration in the history of the world, marked a turning point in the history of steam and the Cunard Line. In 1840 Cunard had begun a transatlantic steamship service for the carriage of mail, supplemented by a few cabin passengers and a modest volume of cargo. The emigration movement changed this almost overnight. The demand for "steerage"—cheap passage—became so great that other steamship companies quickly appeared in response to the need. Cunard would ultimately owe a good deal of his success to profits produced by the carriage of steerage passengers who would provide new blood and enterprise in the New World. In the United States alone, between 1840 and 1900, almost twenty million immigrants arrived by ship from across the Atlantic—more than twice the population of the country at the beginning of that period.

This, then, was the state of the industry when Samuel Cunard settled down in London to devote his time to the steamship company.

However, he would not have long to enjoy this short period of relative calm — the outbreak of the Crimean War in 1854 changed everything.

The last major conflict Cunard had experienced was the Napoleonic War, which ended with the defeat of Napoleon at the decisive Battle of Waterloo in 1815. Although he would not figure in this new conflict, it was Napoleon who said that Constantinople, strategically located at the entrance to the Black Sea in Turkey, was the key to the world. Constantinople provides the clues to understanding the Crimean War.

What started as a diplomatic tussle for influence between Britain, France, and Russia over the weakening Ottoman Empire turned into war in the Near East, focused on the Crimean Peninsula. Russia had for some time been looking at Constantinople, for it would allow its navy access into the Mediterranean Sea and a secure retreat into the Black Sea from any pursuing enemy. Control of this ancient city would have provided Russia with a back door into the Balkans and extended its influence eastward throughout the Levant and the Holy Land as far as Egypt.

By 1850 it had become clear that the Concert of Europe would never permit Russia to take Constantinople; Austro–Hungary because of its proximity to the Balkans, France because of its Near East ambitions, and Great Britain because of its concern for the trade-related avenues to India. Regardless, in 1853 Russia occupied the Turkish Principalities, resulting in war between Turkey and Russia. By the following year that war was going badly for Turkey. Britain and France made a joint demand upon Russia to withdraw, Russia refused, and both Britain and France then joined Turkey in the war over the Crimean Peninsula.

The governments of Britain and France were not prepared for this war; it was fought not for economic interests but rather national ambition, rivalry, and fear. In fact, the conflict with Russia might never have occurred had it not been for "war fever" and national sentiment in Britain's general population.

By June 1854, after the allies had amassed their armies on the Crimea, Russia withdrew its troops from the Turkish Principalities without firing a shot. The original reason for going to war was disposed of—an anti-climax to the previous months of war fever and high-pitched oratory. Back home in England, Prime Minister Palmerston, bolstered by an aggressive press that insisted that the allies attack and occupy Sebastopol, Russia's port city, adopted the same position as the war-mongering press. He urged British troops into armed battle arguing that the "eye-tooth of the bear must be drawn," believing that he represented the British people, to whom withdrawing from the Crimea without having inflicted a drubbing on the Muscovites was intolerable.

War-mongering Britain was lucky to have Samuel Cunard in its midst. Without his help, the Crimean War might have had quite a different result. The Crimea was a great distance from Great Britain, and all troops, equipment, and supplies had to be moved by ship. Success or failure ultimately depended on the transportation of men and materials to the battle zone. With the outbreak of the Crimean War in 1854, the British Government organized their first large-scale movement of troops overseas since the introduction of steam.

The British Admiralty had limited experience with steam and little knowledge of the intricacies of steam transport. While his postal contract with the British Admiralty provided for the use of his ships in the time of conflict, Samuel Cunard shrewdly offered his ships to the government with "no haggle of price, no driving of good bargain." In its disorganized state, the British government was only too happy to accept his offer. It supported Cunard partly because of the strong recommendations from naval and military officers about the fitness of Cunard vessels for war and their more efficient convertibility into men-of-war than any other vessels under contract with the Admiralty.

Having placed his ships at the service of the British government, Cunard devoted his time to advising the Admiralty about obtaining and adapting other steamships for war service. He and his Scottish partners had by then years of experience in arranging and meeting schedules, estimating fuel requirements, outfitting ships for passengers and cargo—in effect, all the skills needed to execute a plan for transporting British troops and equipment to the Crimea. Fourteen Cunard steamers, virtually the entire fleet, were made available to the British Admiralty. These vessels were quickly converted into troopships and transports, some within a week of their return from America. The *Niagara*, the *Cambria*, the *Europa*, the *Etna*, and the *Jura* were fitted out to rush troops to the Mediterranean. The *Arabia* was equipped to carry enormous cargoes of horses, slung in hammocks. The *Alps* and the *Andes* became hospital ships, while some of the other ships engaged in the transportation of French troops.

A mightier armada had never ridden the sea. In six parallel lines, transports, carrying materials and equipment and towed in pairs by the loaded steamers, moved along slowly but imposingly at four knots per hour. The route took the convoy across the English Channel and through the entire length of the Mediterranean Sea to the Crimea and Russian soil. Extensive planning was required to provide sufficient fuel for the ships as well as food for the troops and horses for the lengthy journey.

The extent to which Cunard was involved and the degree of reliance placed upon him during the war is evident from correspondence between Cunard and the Admiralty. For the first eighteen months of the war, the task of overseeing the deployment of troop carriers and transports fell to Sir Alexander Milne, Superintendent Lord of the Great Transport Service. A series of letters from Cunard to Milne during the formative early months of the war provides us with a clear image of Cunard, a man completely in charge and entirely unfazed by the enormity of his task or the responsibility of his position.

February 23, 1854
Dear Captain Milne,

I think you now have a list of every available steamship in the Kingdom suited to your purpose.

If you had rushed into the market you would have paid 100,000 pounds more than you have paid without getting any additional tonnage, beside establishing an extravagant rate of freight for the future.

Other steamships may be dropping in which you may obtain, but not to any great extent. The steamers you have already taken up will be back in three weeks and ready to perform another voyage which will be more advantageous than taking up a great steam fleet at once, even if the ships could be obtained.

I daresay it has not escaped your attention that it would be impossible to have a supply of coal at Malta and other ports in the Mediterranean to meet the demand of so many steamers at once. I will keep you informed of any steamers that may come.

Yours Truly,

S. Cunard

March 15, 1854

Dear Captain Milne,

In your statement of the cost to the government of employing steamships for the conveyance of troops and horses (which in fact could not have been procured in the Kingdom at any price), you have very much under-rated the expense. For example, the Niagara took on board at Malta 630 tons of coal to bring her back to Liverpool which was not a ton more than was absolutely necessary—you estimate the quantity at 480 tons.

The price of coal now at Malta is just what the holders of it may think fit to charge—say, from 4 to 6 pounds per ton—and if you had not sent out more steamers, they must have remained at Malta until coal could have been imported from England by sailing ships.

I have repeatedly heard it said that the horses should have been sent by steam—this circumstance alone will show the impossi-

bility of doing so. [This was in reference to a specific journey; many horses were transported by steam.]
Yours truly,
S. Cunard

May 19, 1854
Dear Captain Milne,
Sir James Graham replied in the House of Commons to questions regarding steamers in the Crimea. The Great Britain broke down a few days after leaving Liverpool so your horses would still be in England if we had hired her.

A reading of this correspondence suggests that the British Admiralty had only limited knowledge of the fuel requirements, availability, and cost of supply of steamships. Milne deferred to Samuel Cunard on these matters—the Admiralty mindset was still geared to sail. In his advisory role Cunard became both instructor and provider of the great transport service. His honest and straightforward writing leaves little room for argument, and his comments in reference to some of the transports suggest a thorough understanding of their construction and suitability for certain types of employment in the transport service, as well as a keen sense of the costs associated with fitting out and converting the ships. In a letter towards the end of this series of letters, not published here, Milne attempts to utilize Cunard's overseas contacts in Boston and New York to secure supplies, both cities being ports regularly frequented by Cunard steamships during their peacetime transatlantic schedule. The correspondence did not continue long, however; with the fall of the Russian fortress at Sebastopol in September of 1855, the Crimean War virtually came to an end. A peace treaty was signed in Paris March 30, 1856.

Initially Cunard's canny Scottish partners may have thought him too generous in so quickly offering virtually the entire Cunard fleet to the Admiralty. However, Cunard knew exactly what he was doing.

Despite the fact that his best vessels were taken out of transatlantic service at a time when the competition with the American Collins Line was gaining momentum, Cunard managed to retain the company's position on the North Atlantic and at the same time do well financially with the chartering of liners for use as transports. The Cunard steamers proved more efficient than the government vessels specifically designed for this service. The company and Samuel Cunard in particular gained invaluable respect from within the British government and the Admiralty for the effective manner in which Cunard and his ships performed during the war. Cunard had conclusively demonstrated the need for and the effectiveness of ocean liners during wartime.

Unfortunately, the Crimean War was not the last conflict to demonstrate the importance of arrangements whereby government subsidized construction of steamships in return for the use of the same ships in periods of armed conflict. As commendable as the performance of the Cunard ships was in the Crimean War, it paled in comparison to the contribution made by Cunard liners in the world wars of the twentieth century, long after Cunard's death.

World War One was the greatest test for the transport services, as war had never before been waged on such a scale, and the Cunard Line assumed an important role. In 1914–1918 Cunard liners transported more than 900,000 officers and soldiers, not including repatriated troops, and more than seven million tons of foodstuffs and war supplies across the hostile North Atlantic. The company paid a stiff price, losing twenty-two vessels in the process.

World War Two provided yet another opportunity for Cunard to contribute, albeit posthumously, towards global peace. Had Britain not had access to fleets of liners, the war would have proceeded quite differently and perhaps had a different outcome. Africa may not have been freed, nor could American troops have been brought so readily to Britain. Of the 151 British passenger ships converted into troopships, some thirty-eight were lost. The majority of those belonged to the Cunard Line, which lost half of its fleet in the conflict.

Although many Cunard ships distinguished themselves while serving as troopships during this war, the *Queen Mary* and *Queen Elizabeth* are accorded the highest praise. Between 1939 and 1945 these two grand liners collectively transported one and a quarter million troops, between them making over sixty round trips on the North Atlantic alone. Sir Winston Churchill, in recognizing the exemplary contribution of the Cunard "Queens" proclaimed that "without their aid, the day of final victory must have unquestionably have been postponed." The performance of these two ships alone is credited with shortening the war by as much as one full year.

Despite advances in technology that have become commonplace in the years since World War Two, it was to the Cunard Line that the British Admiralty turned for assistance in the Falklands Islands campaign of 1982. Times had changed. There were no longer many British passenger ships able to carry a large number of troops over the thousands of miles of storm-tossed ocean that separated England from the Falkland Islands; the Cunard flagship *Queen Elizabeth 2* was one of the few liners available. It was offered for service and converted from an elegant ocean liner to a troopship in only eleven days. It was then able to accommodate 3,150 troops, and departed Southampton on May 12, 1982, with the entire Fifth Infantry Brigade aboard.

Cunard, of course, never lived to see how the experience gained through his contribution in the Crimean War would be employed to shorten hostilities and ensure victory in subsequent conflicts. But the British and French troops were repatriated from the Crimea, Cunard, through his steamships, had once again assumed a prominent role on the world stage.

On March 9, 1859, a grateful nation and the office of its reigning monarch, Queen Victoria, bestowed the title of baronet upon the Steam Lion from Nova Scotia. The recommendation had come from the British Prime Minister Lord Palmerston in recognition of the valuable services rendered by the steamship line, particularly during the Crimean War. The grant of baronetcy was formally presented by

Her Royal Highness "to Samuel Cunard of Bush Hill in the County of Middlesex, Esquire...a man...eminent for family inheritance estate and integrity of manners to and into the dignity state and decree of Baronet."

With the baronetcy came the privilege of acquiring a coat of arms. Cunard received his grant of arms from the College of Heralds on February 28, 1859. The crest features three anchors crowned by a falcon perched on a rock with wings expanded. Fittingly, the motto below reads simply "By Perseverance." Truer words were never spoken to describe the character of this man.

Henceforth he would be referred to as Sir Samuel Cunard. At seventy-two years of age Cunard had now attained standing as a member of the British aristocracy. If he were to choose the pinnacle of his career, this would be the defining moment.

Still, Cunard never lost sight of his own roots in Nova Scotia. His remaining years would be spent endeavouring to improve the lot of the Maritime Provinces from within the circles of government in Westminster.

CHAPTER 12

A Very Good
Kind of Man

U pon moving to London, Cunard had first lived at Bush Hill House, Edmonton, on the Old North River Road overlooking the Lea Valley—about eight miles north of London Bridge. He spent the remaining years of his life in England, often surrounded by his family, many of whom had by then taken up residence in Britain. His youngest girls, Isabella and Elizabeth, had been the last of his daughters to leave Halifax, where they had been living with and caring for Grandmother Duffus. Isabella, following her marriage to Captain Henry Holden in 1850, had moved to Nottingham, not far from the home of her sister Margaret and her husband, Captain William Mellish in the Midlands. When Grandmother Duffus died on January 6, 1858, at the age of eighty-six, Elizabeth moved to London to be with her father. She would stay there until she married Thomas Wilson at Nun Moncton, Yorkshire, on April 30, 1868. William was the last of Cunard's children to live in Halifax, where he remained to oversee the affairs of S. Cunard and Company.

Cunard's move from his native Halifax to England was the result of the evolution of an expanding business empire, coupled with family demographics. Although some perceived his move to England as an act of expatriation, this was not the case. Quite the contrary, by relocating, Cunard was "a British subject who had simply moved from the perimeter to the hub of the Empire, the invariable destiny of the successful in a colonial society." Now, as a highly respected member of the British aristocracy, Samuel Cunard used his well-honed diplomatic skills and influence to better the condition of the colonies in the few years remaining before Confederation.

In the years leading up to and following the creation of the steamship company in 1839, Cunard had carefully cultivated relationships within the highest echelons of British business and government. Many of these acquaintances had been made and fostered years earlier in Halifax, where S. Cunard and Company rose to prominence and attracted attention in the Mother Country. During that time Cunard fashioned his natural business talents, quick perceptions, shrewd judgment, and excellent address — all characteristics that made it easy for him to make and keep friends. He was seldom intimidated by rank or position, and was comfortable with the Halifax military and the navy elite. Through his connections he gained great influence with people in high places in England, including the nobility. Friendships, once made, were seldom lost, but rather nurtured and expanded.

An incident in 1850 involving the loss of the coastal paddle steamer *Orion* off Portpatrick, Scotland, illustrates Cunard's willingness to help a friend in need and also his influence with the British Admiralty. George Burns of Glasgow was one of Cunard's partners as well as an owner of the Glasgow and Liverpool Steam Packet Company. The *Orion*, one of its modern steamers, struck bottom and sank in shallow water off the southwest coast of Scotland in June 1850. Tragically, Burns lost both a brother and niece in this accident. He approached Cunard to determine whether he could use his influence with the Admiralty to help raise the ship. Cunard was quick to respond. Writing the secretary of the Admiralty from the Burlington Hotel, London, on June 25, 1850, Cunard presented the case for his friend Burns:

If a readiness and willingness to assist the distressed, under any and all circumstances should constitute a claim to consideration, there is no person in the world more entitled to consideration than Mr. Burns, and I hope it may be in the power of the Lords of the Admiralty to afford the assistance he now stands in need of.

The response from the Admiralty was immediate. Cunard received a letter the very same day from the secretary of the Admiralty advising that:

My Lords are glad to have it in their power to afford any assistance to Mr. Burns, whose ready service on the occasion of Her Majesty's visit to the West Highlands, as well as his valuable aid in carrying out the relief service in Ireland are fresh in their Lordship's recollection.

Cunard, by virtue of his success as a colonial merchant followed by his spectacular entry into British commercial scene with his steamship enterprise, had become a trusted advisor to the British government on colonial affairs by the time he moved to England. He was well known to the Admiralty and the lords of the Treasury through negotiations for both the original and subsequent postal contracts. He had gained their respect through the strength of his own character—many would later say that he had the ability to make men bend to his will—and through his correspondence which was always clear, courteous, and firm. Cunard asserted his position with dignity, at all times evincing sound business sense and demonstrating his great ability and diplomacy in difficult negotiations. In his latter years Cunard became an advisor to the British government on many matters pertaining to colonial affairs, including immigration, transportation, and the regulation of land ownership.

As early as 1847, Cunard had been called upon to give evidence to the committee of the British House of Lords appointed to consider the subject of emigration from Ireland to the colonies. His views and advice were given considerable weight, as suggested by a newspaper of the day, which reported: "the opinions of a man like Mr. Cunard, upon this enterprise, worthy of the Age and of the British Empire, are of great value."

Cunard spoke in support of the building of a railroad to connect Halifax to Quebec, both to create opportunities for development and to foster unity. In advising the House of Lords, he said: "I think it would be of the greatest national importance the union of the provinces; it would be the means of preserving the provinces and enable you to bring down the produce to the shipping ports in the winter when it would otherwise be shut up in the ice."

Cunard, who by 1860 had become the largest and most influential land proprietor and landlord in Prince Edward Island, was favoured by the British government as the landlords' spokesperson. The subject of non-resident, or absentee, ownership was a hot political issue in PEI at that time. Relations between landlords and tenants had deteriorated over the years, with rent arrears being the primary cause of discord. Cunard alone had 999-year leases with almost a thousand tenants in sixteen townships with terms of one shilling per acre. His agent, George W. Deblois, was finding it increasingly difficult to collect rent, and by 1860 rental arrears due the Cunard estate alone exceeded seventeen thousand pounds.

When the local Island legislature requested a special land commission to settle disputes between landlords and tenants, the Island governor, the Duke of Newcastle, consulted Cunard about appointments to the proposed commission. Once constituted, the commission investigated, and in its report published in the local newspapers, it recommended the implementation of a system of compulsory sale by arbitration, which would extend the application of the Land Purchase Act of 1853 throughout the entire province. Writing to the governor from London on October 2, 1861, Cunard was quick to point out the inequity and inherent weakness of the commission's recommendation. There was no ambiguity in the words and phrases he chose to express his views on the subject:

Assuming the publication [the local newspaper], which is stated to be semi-official is correct, I have to request that Your Grace will permit me, as one of the largest proprietors on the Island to submit a few remarks for your information.

It is reported that, by the award of the commissioners the tenant, although he has taken a lease from my Agent on the terms set forth may compel me to have his farm valued by arbitrators and then take it at the price they fix. I will endeavour to show Your Grace that this clause is illegal and would be ruinous to the proprietor.

Using simple math, Cunard then illustrated that the costs associated with appraisals would be prohibitive and the resulting forced sale detrimental to the landlord and tenant relationship. He concluded by stating:

It appears to me not only to be illegal and fatal to the interests of the proprietors, but so certain to produce litigation between landlord and tenant, that I trust Your Grace will excuse my having submitted my view to your notice. I have not been able to see any of the other proprietors or I should have requested them to join me in this remonstrance to Your Grace.

Cunard's parting words of practical advice to the Governor were to suggest that he "send the bill by packet on Saturday next so it could be passed by the Legislature [in the United Kingdom] this session; otherwise there will be another year of agitation."

Newcastle vetoed the Island assembly's attempt to implement the commissioner's proposals. The matter continued to fester. A subsequent compromise proposal put forth by Cunard in consultation with the proprietors was refused by the executive council of Prince

Edward Island. Landlords, including Cunard, found it increasingly difficult to collect their rents during the ensuing agitation sparked by the Tenant League. At this time Cunard wrote the Colonial Office, saying bluntly, "there is no tenant on the Island who cannot pay his rent if he is industrious and sober," and pointing out that "while the agitation is kept up by designing people, rent will not be paid nor money laid up to purchase farms; time is wasted and money spent in attending political meetings."

In England, the Colonial Office adopted Cunard's stance that neither the Island legislature nor the British government should interfere with his property "in any manner different from that in which private estates in England could be dealt with." Cunard eventually owned one-seventh of the landmass of Prince Edward Island. He had always been interested in land acquisition, more for its timber than for speculative purposes. His leases generally reserved to him all timber and other trees fit for shipping, shipbuilding or exportation. After his death, his estate acceded to the wishes of the provincial government and sold the Cunard land holdings in PEI to the provincial government. Finally the family was clear of the land ownership issue.

Cunard did not live long enough in England to acquire a large circle of friends. He often had differences with his original partners over management of the Cunard Line, and though he maintained cordial relations with Napier, Burns, and MacIver, differences in business style kept them apart socially. Cunard and George Burns, for instance, had ongoing disagreements over company policies. The focus of their dischord was the issue of screw propellors versus paddlewheels. By 1858, Cunard Line was the only company still employing paddlewheels on the Atlantic. Burns held the view that the company was behind the times and was losing out to the competitors, but Cunard had always maintained the policy of only adopting new technology once it was tested and proven perfect by others. He held steadfast to his opinion that paddlewheels looked safer and were preferred by passengers, and neither he nor Burns could be convinced to relinquish their contrary positions on the subject. Their differences precipitated the retirement from the firm by Burns, whose place was taken by his sons, John and James. Until the day he died, Cunard could not erase the memory of this strained friendship. Just hours before he passed away, Cunard arranged with his son Edward to send Burns a letter, which in part read:

> He has within the last week spoken of you in the strongest terms of affection, and referred to years long past. Through all the troubles and vexations which afterwards sprang up, he has never ceased to entertain the same regard for you and Mrs. Burns and John and Jamie.

Samuel's brother Joseph, who had moved to Liverpool, England, after the Miramichi failure of Joseph Cunard and Company, had by this time successfully established himself in that city in the ship agency business, but Samuel only saw him infrequently; their relationship had never really been the same since the Miramichi affair. Despite his failings, Joseph was well liked. The *London Times* paid tribute to his "genial disposition, invariable courtesy and goodness of heart."

Apart from other members of his own immediate family, Cunard occasionally visited with friends from home. The judge and author Thomas Chandler Haliburton, father-in-law to Cunard's son William, was a frequent visitor to Cunard's home at Bush Hill. Haliburton married an English widow, Sarah Harriett Williams, on September 30, 1856, and together they moved into Gordon House, at Islesworth on the Thames River near Twickenham. Samuel visited here with Haliburton, who also lived out his remaining years as a member of the British aristocracy.

Of the opposite sex, Cunard saw even less. Samuel had been a widower since his wife's death in 1828. Perhaps his life was too full to allow him to even contemplate another relationship. He was not unattractive to women, nor did he lack the opportunity to see them romantically. In 1839, while in England to negotiate details for the steamboat service, he had attracted the attention and favour of London's reigning beauty, Caroline Norton. She was a member of the well-known literary family that included the playwright and politician Richard Brinsley Sheridan, and her own father, poet Thomas Sheridan. Following family tradition, Caroline also became a writer, of satire, novels, and popular songs. She was unhappily married to George Norton, an English barrister by profession and a brother of Fletcher Norton, Lord Grantley. Their marriage broke down and a spectacular divorce case ensued, in which George Norton alleged his wife to have committed adultery with the British prime minister, Lord Melbourne. The prime minister was one of many prominent political and social acquaintances with whom Caroline mixed in the fashionable London society. Through her urging, Lord Melbourne had actually arranged to get an appointment of magistrate for Caroline's husband. The grounds for the divorce were not proven and the action failed.

While Cunard was in London obtaining the mails contract, Caroline Norton entertained him and used all her influence to ensure that he met politicians and government officials who might help in his steamship venture. An account of one dinner party hosted by Caroline Norton, then thirty-one years of age, was written up later by Fanny Kemble, the famous American actor and author who was also a guest at the dinner:

> Mrs. Norton maintained her supremacy of beauty and wit in the great London world, and I remember her asking us to dine at her uncle's [Charles Sheridan] when among the people we met were Lord Landsdowne and Lord Normanby, both then in the ministry, whose goodwill and influence she was exerting herself to captivate in behalf of a certain shy, silent, rather rustic gentleman from the far-away province of New Brunswick [Nova Scotia], Mr. Samuel Cunard...of the great mail packet line of steamers between England and America. He had come

to London an obscure and humble individual, endeavouring to procure from the government the sole privilege of carrying the transatlantic mails for his line of steamers. Fortunately for him he had some acquaintance with Mrs. Norton, and the powerful beauty, who was kind-hearted and good-natured...exerted all her interest with her admirers in high places in favour of Cunard, and had made this dinner for the express purpose of bringing her provincial protégé into pleasant personal relations with Lord Landsdowne and Lord Normanby, who were likely to be of great service to him in the special object which had brought him to England.

Just how much influence Caroline Norton had on Cunard's success with the postal contract is a matter of some conjecture. Certainly it did not hurt his cause to have the attention and support of one of the leading bright lights and beauties of London society, who had both the eye and ear of London's political and social elite.

Cunard's acquaintance with Caroline Norton was indirectly the result of relationships he had garnered within Halifax social circles. There, another brother of George Norton and Lord Grantley, Charles Frances Norton, was military secretary to Sir Colin Campbell, lieutenant-governor of Nova Scotia. Charles Norton was born in 1807 and was the same age as his sister-in-law, Caroline Norton. He was married to Sir Colin Campbell's eldest daughter, but succumbed to pneumonia and died at Halifax in 1835 at the age of twenty-eight. He was well known and highly respected by the officers of the Halifax garrison and also by Samuel Cunard. It was Campbell who provided Cunard with the letter of introduction to the British Admiralty in support of Cunard's bid for the postal contract. Cunard's acquaintance with her brother-in-law in Halifax helped to foster a relationship and endear Cunard to Caroline Norton.

Still, the relationship with Caroline did not, as far as historical documentation can tell us, go much further. Cunard remained relatively isolated in London, and kept his widower's existence intact.

Cunard retired in 1863, and his eldest son, Edward, replaced him as the steamship company's senior partner. Edward continued working out of the New York office, and like his father before him frequently travelled between England and America. Meanwhile, his brother William continued to live at Oaklands in Halifax, where he managed the affairs of S. Cunard and Company. Estate planning was already underway, with arrangements made to make apprentices out of Charles and George Francklyn, two sons of Samuel's daughter Sarah.

When Samuel Cunard made his last visit to Halifax, in the summer of 1864, he stayed with William and Laura at Oaklands. He took the opportunity to look about the city of his birth — a place filled with countless memories arising out of a career that spanned seven decades. He visited the old family home at 257 Brunswick Street, and St. Paul's Cemetery, now the Old Burying Ground, opposite St. Matthew's Church on Barrington Street — where his wife, Susan, lay buried.

It was fitting that Cunard returned to England from Halifax that fall aboard the Cunard liner *Scotia*, the last of the Cunard paddle-wheelers and one of the most beautiful ships afloat. Twenty-four years earlier, he had steamed triumphantly into Halifax Harbour aboard the first Cunard steamship, the *Britannia*. So much had changed since then. Now he took his own Atlantic ferry across the ocean one last time.

Soon after returning to England his health deteriorated; he was suffering from respiratory and heart disease. He was then living at Princess Gardens, Kensington. A few months after his return from Halifax he received word that his grandson Arthur, William's son, had died of a fever. Cunard at the time was under doctor's care, and on his advice, the customary Christmas gathering was cancelled. It undoubtedly impacted upon Samuel's health when his brother Joseph died unexpectedly of a heart attack at his home on Upper Liverpool Street in Liverpool on January 16, 1865. Joseph was sixty-five years of age. Samuel's condition worsened. During his last few months he was surrounded by his children, who, through regular correspondence, kept their distant siblings apprised of their father's condition.

April 25, 1865
Dear Jane:
We returned from Norwood Foster-Gateley on Saturday. My father was very well for him but on Sunday at 2:00 a.m. he was taken with a very severe attack of the heart and when got to the house at 2:30 a.m. there seemed to be very little hope of his living from hour to hour—and it was not until later on Sunday that the disease abated and that we had any hope. Yesterday he was much better, but his strength altogether gone. Today he has not been so well as he had a restless night but he is at the moment easier. He is so patient, never uttering a complaint, and even now and then laughing that we have to do everything for him. He has been a kind, good father to us all dear Jane and we will miss him when he is gone...but I trust in God he might be spared a little while.
I write you in a hurry and I will write you tomorrow—I hope that he is improving.
Your affectionate brother,
Edward Cunard

April 26, 1865
My Dear Jane,
My father had a restless night, but he has improved very much today and if he has no relapse will soon be convalescent. Still he is as weak as a baby and the bronchitis holds on. He is so patient and thoughtful, so afraid of giving trouble and so grateful for what we do for him that I get quite overcome. He has slept pretty quietly today but dreams all the time and when he wakes up he insists upon telling us his dreams, and wonders what can put such things in his head. Laura got here last night which I am glad of. I do not tell him I am writing to you as he

would at once begin to talk which we cannot prevent him from doing and which is very bad for him. I hope to send you a better account shortly.

Your affectionate brother

E. Cunard

[Undated letter]

My Dear Jane,

You will be sorry to hear that Papa has had another attack…I think the worst that he has had yet. We did not think that he would survive it and he himself thought that he would not last much longer. He was attacked on Saturday night and early Sunday morning and the attack did not pass off until Monday. Last night he seemed better and was talking about all kinds of things, but this morning I don't think he is so good. He wakes up when Ned and I are standing near him and with tears in his eyes said "I have been thinking about your dear mother and what a woman she was."

I think he is very ill but he is so strong that he might rally and be alright again…

Willie Cunard

There would be no further news except of Samuel's death. The Steam Lion died at 6:00 p.m. on April 28, 1865. His sons, William and Edward, were both at his side. A few days later he was buried at Brompton Cemetery, Kensington.

When Alexander Graham Bell, the inventor of the telephone, died in 1923, the telephone exchange throughout North America was shut down for one minute out of respect for the great inventor as he was laid to rest overlooking the Bras d'Or Lakes at Baddeck, Nova Scotia. One might have expected the transatlantic crossings of the Cunard Line steamers to be suspended following the founder's death — but passages planned for April 29 were made as scheduled. Samuel Cunard would not have had it any other way.

Strict adherence to timetables was, after all, a hallmark of the
Cunard Line.

British newspapers lamented the passing of a great entrepreneur:

> The career of Samuel Cunard fully proves that an energetic and
> expansive spirit may elevate and enable the ordinary aims of
> commerce, by making them instrumental in the advancement
> of the ends of civilization and in the increase of international
> advantages, and the universal public weal. For these substan-
> tial reasons his name will hereafter be written in the Roll of
> England's "Merchant Princes" who have built up her power by
> the arts of peace no less vigorously than her statesmen and
> commanders by the arts of war.

England was quick to claim Cunard as one of their own, but Nova
Scotia was much more modest about one of its most accomplished
native sons. An obituary appearing in the Halifax press noted that:
"among her many illustrious sons who have conferred honour on
their native land, Nova Scotia will not regard among the least Sir
Samuel Cunard."

Years before, Lewis Bliss, a Halifax merchant, wrote to his brother
Henry, a barrister in London, to introduce Samuel Cunard. His
words perhaps best describe the man:

> I like Cunard and hope you will call on him. He is the most lib-
> eral as well as the most extensively engaged in business of all
> our merchants...he is, I think gentlemanly; he certainly is mild
> and pleasant in his manners, of an apparently equal temper and
> possesses a gentle and not unharmonious voice. In short, I look
> on him as a very good kind of man.

Samuel Cunard died as he had lived—revered by his peers, and
regarded by those who knew him—and many who didn't—as a
"good kind of man." Few could ask for a better epitaph.

EPILOGUE:
THE CUNARD LEGACY

When Samuel Cunard passed away at the age of seventy-seven, he had enjoyed a full life, revered by contemporaries as a merchant prince on both sides of the Atlantic. It had been quite a trip—from his youth spent building a shipping empire on the Halifax waterfront, to his knighthood at Westminster and counsel to the House of Lords in England. Nova Scotia native Sir Samuel Cunard died a maritime legend—the man whose "ocean railway" bridged the North Atlantic with steam.

His estate, valued at some 350,000 pounds sterling, was substantial, but not inordinately large by the standards of the day. Cunard had always been very generous with his money, giving freely and often to his children during his lifetime. His will named his sons Edward and William, and his son-in-law William Mellish, who in fact pre-deceased him in 1864, as executors of the estate. Specific directions were given to the executors to raise "six several sums of 20,000 pounds each" within two years, with one share to be given to each of Cunard's six daughters.

At that time, the eldest, Mary, married to James Horsefield Peters, was still living in Charlottetown, Prince Edward Island. Sarah Jane, who had married Gilbert William Francklyn, was back living at Emscote in Halifax following some years spent living abroad in Ceylon. The remaining daughters—Margaret Ann, married to William Leigh Mellish, Anne Elizabeth, wife of Ralph Shuttleworth Allen, Isabella with her husband Henry Holden, and Elizabeth, as yet unmarried—were all living in England. Elizabeth married Thomas Wilson in 1868.

Cunard left the rest of his estate, including his shares in the Cunard Line, to his two sons. By the time the will was filed with the Court of Probate in Halifax in 1870, William Cunard was the sole executor. Edward died in New York from heart disease on April 6, 1869.

The task of taking Samuel Cunard's place on the board of the Cunard Line initially fell to Edward. As the eldest son, Edward also inherited his father's title and became the second baronet. He did not hold it long. Upon his death at the age of fifty-four, and in keeping with the order of succession, the mantle of baronet then moved to his eldest son, Bache Edward Cunard. In the years that followed, the title passed down through the family and was held by Sir Gordon Cunard (son of Bache), Sir Edward Cunard (son of Gordon), Sir William Samuel Cunard (son of William and Laura Cunard), Sir Henry Palmes Cunard (son of Alick May Cunard and Cecil Palmes) and, finally, Sir Guy Alick Cunard, who died without ever having children, thus ending the baronetcy. By this time direct participation by members of the Cunard family on the board of the steamship company had long since ceased.

Edward's death also changed the fortunes of William Cunard. He and his wife Laura were well settled into their Halifax home Oaklands when they found themselves uprooted with a move to London, where William now assumed responsibility for the Cunard family's place at the boardroom table of the Cunard Line. The original Cunard–Burns–MacIver partnership was now under the management of a new generation. Adding to William's workload was the responsibility of administering both his father's and now brother Edward's estates from London.

The beautiful property overlooking Halifax's Northwest Arm was sold. Management of S. Cunard and Company was turned over to William's cousin, John Morrow, and nephew, George Francklyn, who had apprenticed to the company in anticipation of just such an eventuality. George Francklyn had moved his family into the original Cunard home at 257 Brunswick Street when William and Laura moved into Oaklands. William spent the remainder of his life in London, where he died in 1906 at the age of eighty-one. He had retired many years earlier, and his place on the board was taken up by his son Ernest Haliburton, who remained active until the mid-1920s and was the last of the Cunard family to participate in the steamship company.

Today the company is in its 166th consecutive year of operation. It has grown and evolved in ways that the Halifax founder, even with his great foresight, could not have imagined. The many "Cunard firsts," and the evolution from wood to iron to steel hull, from paddlewheel to screw and now azmithpod propulsion, coupled with Cunard's unmatched record of safety and seamanship, have created the Cunard Tradition, still unchallenged in the annals of ocean liner history. The Cunard Line has been rejuvenated by the new flagship, *Queen Mary 2*, and through it, and the fortunes of the company are secure. It remains the oldest ocean liner company in the world.

Each of the original partners in the company possessed special skills and attributes that led to the Cunard Line's success. Robert Napier produced engines of the highest quality. Cunard liners were built to the most exacting standards, overseen under the meticulous supervision of George Burns. Charles MacIver had a particular talent for ensuring that Cunard vessels were staffed only by the best officers and crew. Cunard masters became legends: names like MacDougall, Judkins, Doyle, Rostron, Bissett, and Warwick are synonymous with the Cunard liners they helped make household names: the *Britannia*, the *Persia*, the *Carpathia*, the *Mauretania*, and the "Queens" — the *Queen Mary*, the *Queen Elizabeth*, the *Queen Elizabeth 2*, the *Queen Mary 2*, and now the *Queen Victoria*, slated for launch in 2007.

Samuel Cunard, of course, brought his own unique talents to the partnership. It is to Samuel Cunard, more than any other individual or circumstance, that the Cunard Line owes its success. From his youth until his dying day, Samuel Cunard practiced steadfast industry, sound judgment, undaunted determination, keen perception, and an unassuming but rock-solid confidence. Throughout his life Cunard endeavoured to serve the public, not take advantage of it. The vast number of organizations and projects to which he gave voluntarily of his time in Halifax alone is testimony to his generosity of spirit. And, for a man whose every waking hour was filled, Cunard had remarkably strong connections to his family.

Samuel Cunard, the Steam Lion, led by example — and in so doing left us with his example to emulate.

APPENDIX 1: SHORT BIOGRAPHIES OF CUNARD FAMILY MEMBERS

Samuel Cunard was a son of Abraham Cunard and Margaret Murphy.

Abraham Cunard was born in Montgomery County, near Germantown, Pennsylvania to Samuel Cunard and Susanna Foulke in or about 1755. While aboard the loyalist ship *Union* in the Spring of 1783, he met Margaret Murphy, whose father Thomas (sometimes referred to as John) had emigrated to South Carolina from Ireland in 1773. Abraham and Margaret were married in Halifax, Nova Scotia June 22, 1783, and took up residence in a small cottage off Brunswick Street in that city. After living most of their married lives in Halifax they retired to Rawdon, Hants County, Nova Scotia. Margaret died there December 28, 1821, followed by Abraham January 10, 1824. Both are buried in the cemetery of St. Paul's Anglican Church, Center Rawdon, Nova Scotia. They produced seven sons and two daughters. A tenth child, a son, died at birth around 1794.

CHILDREN OF MARGARET AND ABRAHAM CUNARD

• Mary was born in Halifax in the year 1784. Little is known of her childhood. She married John Parr, a master mariner from Liverpool, England, in Halifax on August 6, 1803. They had a son, Samuel, and an infant daughter, Margaret Ann. Tragically, mother, father, and daughter died of yellow fever at Bridgetown, Barbados, while John Parr was working on a vessel employed by His Majesty's Transport Services. John succumbed first, passing away January 1, 1811. Mary followed on January 4; their daughter survived for two weeks before expiring on January 19 at the age of only seven months. It appears that their son had died some time before.

• Samuel

• William was born in Halifax about 1789. He played a minor role in the firm A. Cunard and Son. He lived in Halifax and was becoming a respected businessman when he died as a passenger aboard the ship *Wyton*, which was wrecked off Cape North, Cape Breton Island, on November 25, 1824.

• Susan was born in Halifax about 1792. She married John Roy, a Halifax merchant, at St. Matthew's Church on June 4, 1814. Her brother Samuel signed the marriage bond. It was to be a short marriage. Susan died May 4, 1815, after the birth of a daughter, Mary Susan Cunard Roy, who, twenty years later, married Richard Carman of Marysville, New Brunswick.

• Edward was born in Halifax about 1798 and, like most of his siblings, little is known about his youth. He had a small share in the firm A. Cunard and Son after his father Abraham retired to Rawdon. Early on he was master of different sailing vessels owned by his older brother Samuel, and he was registered as the owner of a number of sailing ships, including the brig *Amelia* and the barques *Duke of Wellington, Nereid, Ocean,* and *Thetis.* He married Margaret Jane Yeomans, daughter of Henry Yeomans, town clerk in 1806, and later became an insurance broker. They had a daughter, Emily, and two sons, George and Henry Samuel. Edward was for a time master of the government brig *Chebucto.* In 1835 he was director of the Marine Insurance Company and a commissioner appointed under the Act to Regulate the Pilotage of Vessels at the Port of Halifax. He died on September 11, 1851, at fifty-four. Following his death his widow Margaret continued to live at her home at 120 Morris Street in Halifax until her death on August 15, 1880.

• Joseph was born in Halifax in 1799. He attended Halifax Grammar School and, like some of his other brothers, worked briefly in the firm

A. Cunard and Son. Around 1820, under the direction of older brother Samuel, he went to Miramichi in New Brunswick, where he established a branch of the family shipping business under the name of Joseph Cunard and Company. He was elected to the New Brunswick House of Assembly as member for Northumberland County in 1828, retaining his seat until 1833, when he was appointed to the Legislative Council. He became one of the wealthiest and most influential merchants in the province. On August 15, 1833, he married Mary Peters of Bushville at Chatham, New Brunswick. They had four sons and a daughter. Reckless business practices, overextension, and depressed economic conditions forced Joseph and his company into bankruptcy in 1847. He left Chatham in 1850 and relocated to Liverpool, England, where he entered the ship commission business as partner in the firm Cunard, Munn and Company. In 1855 he formed a new company, Cunard, Brett and Austin, which became Cunard, Wilson and Company in 1857. He lived on Upper Parliament Street in Liverpool, where he died on January 16, 1865.

• John was born in 1800 and took up a life at sea. In 1823 he was master of the brig *Chebucto*, taking supplies to Sable Island, and in 1830 he was master of the schooner *Henrietta* when it was sold in London. He died at the age of forty-four in 1844, never having married. In his will he left a lot and premises at Upper Water Street in Halifax plus sixty-two pounds to Emily Carritt, daughter of William Carritt, a teller at the Bank of British North America. He also provided for a small trust for Henrietta Carritt, William's wife.

• Thomas was very close in age to his brother Joseph. He attended Pictou Academy, along with his younger brother, John. He lived in Halifax and may have worked for a while in the family business. He did not marry. In 1826 he was registered as having a half interest, along with J. H. Tidmarsh, in the 122-ton schooner *Emilia*, lost off Halifax Harbour in December of that year. He appears to have been closest to his brother Henry, as evidenced in his will, in which he left his very modest estate to his "dear brother Henry Cunard." He died in 1828.

• Henry was the baby of the family and lived the longest. He was born in Halifax in 1804, and his early schooling was at Pictou Academy. He initially stayed with his parents to help them with their retirement in Rawdon. Following their deaths, he went to Miramichi to help brother Joseph with Joseph Cunard and Company. On September 30, 1830, he married Elizabeth Duffus, daughter of William and Susannah Duffus and younger sister of Samuel's wife, Susan. They had two children, one of whom, Susannah, died in 1835 at the age of four and is buried in the cemetery at St. Paul's Anglican Church outside Chatham. Around 1842 Henry moved to Woodburn, near Chatham, where he built a house and enjoyed the rest of his years as a gentleman farmer with other modest business interests. He died at Woodburn July 30, 1885, at the age of eighty-one.

CHILDREN OF SAMUEL AND SUSAN CUNARD

• Edward was born at Halifax on December 31, 1815. He was baptized at St. Paul's Church by Reverend George Wright on March 24, 1816. He attended King's College at Windsor, Nova Scotia, and on May 17, 1849, at New York, wed Mary Bache McEvers, daughter of Bache McEvers, a merchant of that city. Edward managed the New York offices of the Cunard Line from his home on Staten Island. He and Mary had eight children: Samuel, who died in infancy, Bache Edward, who became third baronet following his father's death, Mary, Edward, Gordon, who became fourth baronet, Jeanette, Anne, and Caroline Margaret. Bache Edward, born May 15, 1851 attained dubious notoriety when he married a San Francisco socialite, Maud Alice Burke, on April 17, 1895. She had travelled extensively in Europe and married on the rebound from a failed relationship with a Polish Prince. She and Bache had nothing in common. He was much involved in fox hunting and lived in a large estate near Market

Harborough, Leicestershire, for fifteen years. A daughter, Nancy, was born in 1896, and became a well-known social activist in the 1920s and 1930s. Maud Alice Burke left Bache and moved to London. Bache thereafter lived a solitary life, committed to the hunt until his death November 3, 1925.

• Mary, born April 21, 1817, was named after Samuel's sister who died of yellow fever in 1811. She was baptized by Reverend John Inglis, Rector of St. Paul's Church, on May 25, 1817. Little is known about her until September 3, 1837 when she married James Horsefield Peters, a New Brunswick barrister who shortly after became agent in Prince Edward Island for his father-in-law. Mary and her husband moved there and lived in Charlottetown, where they raised a family of six children: Susan Margaret, who died young, Mary Caroline, Thomas Sherman, Frederick, Anthony, and Margaret Laura. Mary died August 11, 1885 at the age of sixty-eight.

• Susan was born February 6, 1819, and named after her mother and maternal grandmother. Baptized at St. Paul's Church by Reverend John Inglis on April 18, 1819, she died on February 2, 1829, at the age of ten.

• Margaret Ann was born in Halifax on March 14, 1820, and named for Samuel Cunard's mother. She was baptized at St. Paul's Church on May 7, 1820, and was married at St. George's Round Church on October 19, 1843, to William Leigh Mellish, captain in His Majesty's Rifle Brigade. They had six children: Edward Leigh, Agnes, William Chambers, Henry, Evelyn, and George. Margaret Ann died December 11, 1901, at the age of eighty-one. She had been a widow for more than thirty-five years, since her husband's death on April 18, 1864.

• Sarah Jane was born at Halifax December 21, 1821. She married Gilbert William Francklyn, a colonel in His Majesty's Thirty-seventh

Regiment. Together they lived at Emscote on the Northwest Arm in Halifax's South End. They had nine children: Margaret Moore, Charles Gilbert, Gladys Elizabeth, George Edward, Frances Mary, Annie Kate, Laura Isabel, Helen Jane, and Edith. A few months before the wedding, on June 4, 1840, Sarah Jane, accompanied by her sister Margaret Anne, helped christen their father's newest sailing vessel, *Thetis*, at the Lyle Shipyard in Dartmouth.

• Anne Elizabeth was born at Halifax on March 25, 1823. She was baptized at St. Paul's Church on June 15, 1823. She was married by the Lord Bishop of Nova Scotia at St. George's Round Church to Ralph Shuttleworth Allen, a lieutenant in the Royal Artillery hailing from Bathampton, England. They produced five children: Ralph Edward, George Cunard, Fanny Mary, Henry, and Philip. Anne and her husband died within one day of each other; she passed away at Bath, England on October 14, 1862.

• William was born in Halifax on April 5, 1825. He was baptized by Reverend B. G. Gray at St. George's Round Church on April 17, 1827. On December 30, 1851, he married Laura Charlotte Haliburton, daughter of Honourable Thomas Chandler Haliburton of Windsor, Nova Scotia. Before building their home on the Northwest Arm, they lived in the family home on Brunswick Street. They raised a family of seven: William Samuel, Ernest Haliburton, Herbert and Arthur (twins, both of whom died in childhood), Cyril Grant, Alice Mary, and Louisa Neville. William managed the affairs of S. Cunard and Company in Halifax following his father's move to London. After his father's death William moved to London, where he continued to reside until his death on January 13, 1906, at age eighty-one. Laura survived him for a few years, dying at Nice, France, on December 30, 1910.

• Isabella was born in Halifax on Valentine's Day in 1827. She was baptized by Reverend B. G. Gray at St. George's Round Church on

April 5, 1827. It was at this same church that she wed Henry Holden, chief constable of Nottinghamshire, England, on October 21, 1850, with Reverend R. J. Uniacke officiating. They had four children: Harry, Maude, Blanche, and Ethel. Isabella died in England March 7, 1894, at the age of sixty-seven.

• Elizabeth was the last child born to Samuel and Susan Cunard, and after giving birth to her, on January 23, 1828, Susan died. Reverend R. F. Uniacke performed the baptism for Elizabeth at St. George's Round Church on June 29, 1829. Elizabeth's father did not live to see her marry. She wed Thomas Wilson at Nun Monckton, Yorkshire, England, on April 30, 1868. They did not have any children. Elizabeth died March 4, 1889, at the age of sixty-one.

APPENDIX 2: PARTIAL LIST OF SAILING VESSELS REGISTERED IN HALIFAX TO SAMUEL CUNARD AND HIS BROTHERS BETWEEN 1815 AND 1840

Vessel	Year - Registration Number	Tons	Rig	Builder	Owner	Master
Admiral Lake	1826 - #343	155	Brig	Robert Knight Douglas, N.S.	S.C.	David Davis
Alante	1824 - #67		Schooner		S.C.	Peter Whalen
Alert	1843 - #104	404	Barque	Alexander Lyle Dartmouth, N.S.	S.C.	
Amelia	1839 - #182	200	Brig	Alexander Lyle Dartmouth, N.S.	E.C.	Joseph Murray
Ann	1830 - #108	91	Brig	William Duffus Bras d'Or Lakes	S.C.	Evander MacLeod
Bainbridge	1831 - #139	429	Ship	Chapel PEI (1826)	S.C.	Nathaniel Levy West
Barbara	1846 - #20	459	Barque	Alexander Lyle Dartmouth, N.S.	S.C.	James MacKay
Brazilian Patriot	1825 - #170	69	Schooner	Petit de Gras, C.B.	S.C.	Lewis Morrow
Britannia	1846 - #144	217	Brig	James Kitchen Sr Pictou, N.S.	S.C.	James MacKay
Catherine	1828 - #169		Brig	Bras d'Or Lakes	S.C.	Richard Browne
Chebucto	1823	134	Brig		S.C.	Edward Cunard
Cherub	1822 - #31	76	Brig	PEI	S.C.	George Kysh
Clarence	1827 - #172	254	Brig	Jacob Utley Clare, N.S.	S.C.	Lancelot Busby
Columbia	1833	393	Ship		S.C.	
Countess of Dalhousie	1817	91	Schooner		S.C.	William Crocker
Cumberland	1846 - #145	386	Barque	James Kitchen River John, N.S.	S.C.	John M. Fraser
Deborah	1847 - #248	624	Barque	Alexander Lyle Country Hbr., N.S.	S.C.	
Duke of Wellington	1840 - #139	268	Barque	William Bent Pugwash, N.S.	E.C.	Edward Cunard

Eclipse	1814 - #101	94	Sloop		S.C.	

Vessel	Year - Registration Number	Tons	Rig	Builder	Owner	Master
Edward	1828 - #188	132	Brig	Lemuel Cambridge PEI	S.C.	Thomas Geo. White
Edward	1839	438	Barque	Angus MacDonald Brudnell Pt. PEI	S.C.	
Eliza	1824 - #145	61	Schooner	John Gosbee Counry Hbr. N.S.	S.C.	John Gosbee
Eliza	1824 - #5	210	Brig	St. Martens, N.B.	S.C.	Edward Cunard
Emilia	1826 - #22		Schooner		T.C.	E. Dillon
Emily	1827 - #12	88	Brig	Richard Burnett St.Peters Bay, N.B.	S.C.	Tom Hughes
Empress	1847 - #221	359	Barque	Newport, N.S.	S.C.	
Euterpe	1826 - #371	77	Schooner	Devon, U.K.	S.C.	Duncan MacNicoll
Fame	1826 - #79	125	Brig	Argyle, N.S.	S.C.	Jasper Rutter
Frederica	1845 - #85	222	Brig	Lunenburg, N.S.	S.C.	Jasper Rutter
George	1827 - #137	114	Schooner	Shediac, N.B.	S.C.	Abraham Taylor
George Canning	1827 - #142	265	Brig	William Dickson Truro, N.S.	S.C.	Charles Marshall
Henrietta	1826 - #280	152	Schooner	St. John, N.B.	S.C.	John Cunard
James	1833 - #202	358	Barque	Cocagne, N.B.	S.C.	Robert Long
Jane	1822 - #75	83	Brig	Pictou, N.S.	S.C.+	David Davis
Jane	1830 - #170	268	Barque	Clare, N.S.	S.C.	John Price
Jane	1830 - #176	146	Brig	Miramichi, N.B.	S.C.	Simon Dodd
Jane	1834 - #165	142	Brig		S.C.	
Jessie	1826 - #323	345	Brig	Pictou, N.S.	S.C.	Edward Cunard
John	1828 - #49	90	Schooner	Samuel Theriault Annapolis, N.S.	S.C.	Edward Cunard
John Bainbridge	1826 - #128	365	Barque	James Cain Bras d'Or, N.S.	S.C.	Edward Cunard
Kate	1832 - #126	140	Brig	Josiah Davidson	S.C.	John Winn

Vessel	Year - Registration Number	Tons	Rig	Builder	Owner	Master
Lady Lilford	1838 - #140	596	Ship	Parrsboro, N.S. Alexander Lyle Dartmouth, N.S.	S.C.	James Galt
Lady Ogle	1827 - #150	115	Schooner	Robert Knight Douglas, N.S.	S.C.	Thomas Wilson

Vessel	Year - Registration Number	Tons	Rig	Builder	Owner	Master
Lady Paget	183 - #235	500	Barque	Alexander Lyle Dartmouth, N.S.	S.C.	James Galt
Lady Sarah Maitland	1828 - #206	139	Schooner	Lemuel Cabridge PEI	S.C.	William Stairs
Lady Strange	1828 - #53	118	Schooner	William Freize Truro, N.S.	S.C.	Edward Cunard
London	1825 - #139	202	Brig	Hylton, U.K.	S.C.	Vaud Cuthbert
Margaret	1826 - #223	832	Brig	Tergenmouth Devon, U.K. 1814	S.C.	
Margaret	1826 - #201	47	Schooner	Pictou, N.S. 1823	E.C.	David Davis
Margaret	1826 - #304	133	Schooner		S.C.	Lewis Morris
Margaret	1827 - #1	265	Brig		S.C.	David Davis
Margaret	1834 - #162	626	Barque	Darmouth, N.S.	S.C.	
Maria	1833 - #100		Brig	Alexander Lyle Dartmouth, N.S.	S.C.	David Buchan
Marmion	1827 - #29	135	Brig	PEI	S.C.	William Skinner
Mary & Betsy	1818 - #22	108	Sloop	"prize"	S.C.	
Mary	1839 - #252	450	Barque	Alexander Lyle Dartmouth, N.S.	E.C.	James H. Godfrey
Mary Ann	1824 - #22	97	Brig	Magdeline Is.(1819)	S.C.	John Stairs
Nereid	1841 - #151	672	Barque	Alexander Lyle Dartmouth, N.S	E.C.	Thomas Poole
Ocean	1840 - #225	560	Barque	Alexander Lyle Dartmouth, N.S.	E.C.	James Daly
Pacific	1827 - #9	402	Ship	Robert Louden Dartmouth, N.S.	S.C.+	George Pyke
Pacific	1834 - #174	202	Ship	"altered"		
Pocahontas	1831 - #112	55	Schooner	Alexander Lyle Dartmouth, N.S.	S.C.	David and Francis Heard
Prince of	1824 - #40	142	Brig	"prize"	S.C.	David Davis

Waterloo						
Queen	1823 - #7	71	Brig	Argyle, N.S.	S.C.	Duncan MacNicoll
Rose	1829 - #148	416	Ship	Brighthelmsea,UK 1806	S.C.	Samuel Hain
Rose	1833 - #19	416	Ship		S.C.	Edward Cunard
Rose	1833 - #171	421	Barque	"altered"	S.C.	

Vessel	Year - Registration Number	Tons	Rig	Builder	Owner	Master
Rebecca	1818 - #87	29	Schooner	Lunenburg, N.S.	S.C.	
Robust	1817 - #99	42	Schooner	Lunenburg, N.S.	S.C.	
Samuel Cunard	1827 - #162	303	Ship	William Duffus Big Bras d'Or, N.S.	S.C.	Findlayson
Sarah	1832 - #125	151	Barque	Cocagne, N.B.	S.C.	Simon Graham
Sea	1842 - #106	125	Brig	Miramichi, N.B.	Boggs	
Sir Walter Scott	1826 - #363	218	Brig	James Dawson Pictou, N.S.	S.C.	Edward Cunard
Shubenacadie	1825 - #144	178	Brig	Shubenacadie, N.S.	S.C.	W. Cocken
Sophia	1828 - #14	106	Brig	Phinneas Lovett Annapolis, N.S.	S.C.	Edward Cunard
Susan	1823 - #38	106	Brig	Leppert Halifax, N.S.	S.C.	Edward Cunard
Susan	1843 - #126	106	Brig	Miramichi, N.B.	S.C.	
Susan & Sarah	1830 - #143	329	Ship	Sissibo, N.B.	S.C.	Simon MacLean
Sybyllia	1833 - #18	325	Ship		S.C.	Simon Graham
Thetis	1840 - #105	584	Barque	Alexander Lyle Dartmouth, N.S.	E.C.	James Wade
Thornley	1822 - #65	155	Brig	Hylton, UK (1813)	S.C.	Edward Cunard
Trial	1830 - #114	75	Schooner	New London, PEI	S.C.	William Bigelow
True Blue	1827 - #40	100	Brig	Bedeque, PEI	S.C.	Malcolm Douglas
Velocity	1818 - #36	133	Brig	Bridgport, UK	S.C.	Richard Stewart

				(1811)		
Volant	1825 - #72	65	Schooner	Shelburne, N.S.	S.C.	John MacNeil
William	1828 - #130	268	Brig	Shediac, N.B.	S.C.	Edward Cunard
William the Fourth	1833 - # 90		Brig	Truro, N.S.	S.C.	Alexander Henry

SELECTED BIBLIOGRAPHY

BOOKS:

Armstrong, Warren. *Atlantic Highway.* New York: The John Day Company, 1962.

Arnell, J. C. *Steam and the North Atlantic Mails: The Impact of the Cunard Line and Subsequent Steamship Companies On the Carriage of Transatlantic Mails.* Toronto: The Unitrade Press, 1986.

Babcock, F. Lawrence. *Spanning the Atlantic.* New York: Alfred A. Knopf, 1931.

Barnett, Donna. *River of Dreams: The Saga of the Shubenacadie Canal.* Halifax: Nimbus Publishing, 2002.

Bassett, John M. *Samuel Cunard (The Canadians).* Don Mills, Ontario: Fitzhenry and Whiteside Ltd., 1976.

Beck, J. Murray. *Joseph Howe, Volume 1: Conservative Reformer 1804–1848.* Montreal: McGill-Queen's University Press, 1982.

Blakeley, Phyllis. "Samuel Cunard," in *Dictionary of Canadian Biography.* Vol. IX. , 172–186.

Bonsor, N.R.P. *North Atlantic Seaway, An Illustrated History of the Passenger Services Linking the Old World with the New in Five Volumes.* Jersey, Channel Islands: Brookside Publications, 1980.

Brinnin, John Malcolm. *The Sway of the Grand Saloon.* New York: Delacorte Press, 1971.

Budge, Billy. *Memoirs of a Lightkeeper's Son: Life on St. Paul Island.* East Lawrencetown, Nova Scotia: Pottersfield Press, 2003.

Butler, Daniel Allen. *The Age of Cunard.* Annapolis, MD: Lighthouse Press, 2003.

Cameron, James M. *Pictou County's History.* New Glasgow, Nova Scotia: Pictou County Historical Society, 1972.

Chisholm, Anne. *Nancy Cunard.* New York: Alfred A. Knopf, 1979.

Croil, James. *Steam Navigation: Its Relation to Commerce of Canada and United States.* Toronto: William Briggs, 1898.

Davies, Richard A. *The Letters of Thomas Chandler Haliburton*. Toronto: University of Toronto Press, 1988.

Dennis, Clara. *Cape Breton Over*. Toronto: The Ryerson Press, 1942.

Elsna, Hebe. *Mrs. Melboure*. London: Collins Clear-Type Press, 1956.

Encyclopedia Britannica, Eleventh Edition. New York, 1910.

Fielding, Daphne. *Emerald & Nancy: Lady Cunard and Her Daughter*. London: Eyre and Spottiswoode, 1968.

Fiftieth Anniversary of Royal Bank of Canada (1869-1919). Montreal: The Ronalds Press and Advertising Agency Ltd., 1920.

Fraser, James A. *By Favourable Winds: A History of Chatham*. New Brunswick: Town of Chatham, 1975.

Grant, Kay. *Samuel Cunard: Pioneer of the Atlantic Steamship*. New York: Abelard-Schuman, 1967.

Hamilton, William B. "George Wright," in *The Dictionary of Canadian Biography V*.

Harris, R.V. *The Church of St. Paul In Halifax, Nova Scotia, 1749–1949*. Toronto: Ryerson Press, 1949.

Hichens, Walter W. *Island Trek: an Historical and Geographical Tour of Seal Island*. Hantsport, Nova Scotia: Lancelot Press, 1982.

Hurd, Archibald. *A Merchant Fleet at War*. London: Cassel and Company, 1920.

Hyde, Francis E. *Cunard and the North Atlantic 1840–1973: A History of Shipping and Financial Management*. London: MacMillan, 1975.

Jackson, Elva E. *Windows On the Past: North Sydney, Nova Scotia*. Hantsport, Nova Scotia: Lancelot Press, 1974.

Johnson, Edgar. *Charles Dickens: His Tragedy and Triumph*. Vols. 1 and 2. New York: Simon and Schuster, 1952.

Johnson, Howard. *The Cunard Story*. London: Whittet Books, 1987.

Langille, Jacqueline. *Samuel Cunard*. Tantallon, Nova Scotia: Four East Publications, 1992.

— —. *Thomas Chandler Haliburton*. Tantallon, Nova Scotia: Four East Publications Ltd., 1990.

— —. "Samuel Cunard," in *The Haligonians*. Halifax, Nova Scotia: Formac Publishing Company, 2005.

MacDonald, A. Fraser. *Our Ocean Railways or The Rise, Progress and Development of Ocean Steam Navigation*. London: Chapman and Hall, 1893.

Maginnis, Arthur J. *The Atlantic Ferry: Its Ships, Men & Working*. London: Whittaker, 1900.

MacLaren, George. *The Pictou Book*, New Glasgow, N.S., Hector Publishing Company, 1954.

Martin, John Patrick. *The Story of Dartmouth*. Dartmouth: self-published, 1957.

Martin, Lois. *Historical Sketches of Miramichi*. Chatham: self-published, 1985.

Mills, Chris. *Vanishing Lights*. Hantsport, Nova Scotia: Lancelot Press, 1992.

Myatt, Reverend Wilfred E. *Oliver Goldsmith: A Chapter in Canada's Literary History*. 2nd ed. Hantsport, Nova Scotia: Lancelot Press, 1985.

Newell, Sonia. *Seal Island: an Echo from the Past*. Yarmouth: Sentinel Printing, 1988.

Pacey, Elizabeth. *Miracle On Brunswick Street: The Story of St. George's Round Church and the Little Dutch Church*. Halifax, Nova Scotia: Nimbus Publishing, 2003.

Patterson, Reverend George. *History of the County of Pictou*, 1877.

Patterson, George Geddie. *History of Victoria County*. Sydney, Nova Scotia: College of Cape Breton Press, 1978.

Payzant, Joan M., and Lewis J. Payzant. *Like a Weaver's Shuttle: A History of the Halifax-Dartmouth Ferries*. Halifax: Nimbus Publishing, 1979.

Pennypacker, Samuel W. *The Settlement of Germantown Pennsylvania*. Philadelphia: William J. Campbell, 1899.

Quinpool, John. *First Things In Acadia: the Birthplace of a Continent*. Halifax, Nova Scotia: First Things Publishers, 1936.

Regan, John W. *Sketches and Traditions of the Northwest Arm*. Halifax: McAlpine Publishing Company, 1909.

Rigby, Carle A. *St. Paul Island: The Graveyard of the Gulf*. Hartland, New Brunswick: Hartland Publishers Ltd, 1979.

Spratt, H. Philip. *Transatlantic Paddle Steamers*. 2nd ed. Glasgow: Brown, Son and Ferguson, 1967.

Spray, W. A. "Joseph Cunard," in *Dictionary of Canadian Biography*, Vol. 1X.

Staff, Frank. *The Transatlantic Mail*. Lawrence, MA: Quarterman Publications, 1980.

Stephens, David E. *Lighthouses of Nova Scotia*. Windsor, Nova Scotia: Lancelot Press, 1973.

Tute, Warren. *Atlantic Conquest: the Ships and Men of the North Atlantic Passenger Services 1816–1961*. London: Cassel and Company, 1962.

Whitelaw, Marjorie. *Thomas MacCulloch: His Life and Times*. Halifax, Nova Scotia: Nova Scotia Museum, 1985.

Whitney, Dudley. *The Lighthouse*. Toronto: McLelland and Stewart, 1975.

Zinck, Jack. *Shipwrecks of Nova Scotia*. Vol. 1. Hantsport, Nova Scotia: Lancelot Press, 1975.

NEWSPAPERS

Acadian Recorder, February 11, 1813; June 3, 1826; March 13, 1830; August 7, 1830; September 3, 1831; October 24, 1835; August 1, 1840; August 8, 1840; January 22, 1842; November 29, 1890; September 13, 1919.

Advertiser and Patriot, July 20 and 22, 1840.

The Chatham Gleanor, May 2, 1841; June 23, 1840.

Colonial Herald, September 9, 1830.

Colonial Patriot, August 26, 1829; August 13, 1833.

Glasgow Courier, February 6, 1840.

Halifax Mail, February 21, 1931.

Halifax Recorder, January 15, 1927.

The Morning Herald, November 2, 1880; November 13, 1883.

The Nova Scotian, March 11, 1830; April 30, 1830; September 2, 1830;

September 9, 1830; December 23, 1830; September 1, 1831; October 13, 1831; January 24, 1832; May 2, 1833; February 26, 1835; July 16, 1835; September 17, 1835; September 7, 1837; April 11, 1839; August 15, 1839; August 29, 1839; July 23, 1840; August 5, 1840.

Pictou Advocate, November 19, 1936.

The Recorder, April 28, 1917.

The Scotia Sun, August 2, 1978.

The Times (Halifax), November 16, 1847.

Weekly Chronicle (Halifax), July 2, 1813; January 16, 1824.

Yarmouth Herald, May 7, 1836.

OTHER

Aikens, Thomas Beamish. "History of Halifax City," in *Collections* V111, periodical of the Nova Scotia Historical Society, 1895.

An Act to Authorize the Appointing Commissioners for Lighthouses, Nova Scotia Statutes 1816, 56.

Blakeley and Stephens. "Ships of the North Shore (Pictou, Colchester and Cumberland Counties)." Occasional Paper Number 11, Halifax, 1963.

Copp, Ronald Walter. "Nova Scotia Trade During the War of 1812," in *Canadian Historical Review*, number 18, 1937.

Cox, Leo. "A Pioneer of Ocean Navigation." *Canadian Geographical Journal*, March 1935.

Cunard, Samuel. Letters written in his capacity as agent for the General Mining Association. Held at the Beaton Institute, Cape Breton University, Nova Scotia. MG 14, 19, letters 16, 17, 18, 45, 46, 48, 49, 51, 55, 71, 85 and 87.

Evans, Reginald D. "Transportation and Communication in Nova Scotia (1815-1850)." Thesis, 1936.

Gannett, Erza S. *Sermon: The Arrival of the Britannia*. Delivered at the Federal Street Meeting House, Boston, July 1, 1840. Dutton and Wentworth's Steam Press, c.1840.

Gillis, Rannie. "Family Matters: Connecting the past with the present on a remote island off Cape Breton," in *Saltscapes*, March/April 2005.

Harvey, D. C. "Cunard and Steam Communication." Nova Scotia Archives and Records Management, MG1, Vol. 437.

— — —. "Hopes Raised by Steam in 1840." Report of the Canadian Historical Association, 1940.

Heyl, Erik. Article in *Early American Steamers*, Vol. 2, 1956.

Illustrated London News, "Loss of the Columbia Steam-Ship," August 5, 1843.

"Journal and Proceedings of the General Assembly of the Province of Nova Scotia," November 2, 1787.

Langley, John G. "Samuel Cunard: As Fine a Specimen of a Self-made Man as this Western Continent Can Boast Of," in the *Journal of the Royal Nova Scotia Historical Society*, Vol 8. Halifax, 2005.

MacMechan, Archibald. "Samuel Cunard." Booklet. Toronto: The Ryerson Press, 1928.

Manny, Louise. "Old Time Shipping on the Miramichi." Private paper.

— — —. "Ships of Miramichi." Private paper.

— — —. "Collossus of the Miramichi," in *Atlantic Advocate* No. 55, November 1964.

Martell, J.S. "Intercolonial Communications, 1840-1867." Paper for the Canadian Historical Association, 1938.

McNally, Larry. "The Royal William: The Saga of a Pioneering Steam Vessel." *The Archivist*, July-August 1990.

Milne, Sir Alexander. "Papers containing letters between Milne, Admiral of the British Fleet and Samuel Cunard during Crimean War." Nova Scotia Archives and Records Management, MG1, Vol. 3011, files 9 and 10.

The Provincial: Halifax Monthly Magazine, "The Honourable Samuel Cunard & Ocean Steam Navigation," January 1853.

Quinpool, John. "A Century in Steam: the Story of the First Transatlantic Steamship to Dock at a Canadian Port...." Private paper, 1940.

Reford, R.W. "A Great Canadian-Sir Samuel Cunard." Pamphlet. August 4, 1924.

Robertson, R.G. "Tracing the History of British Warships in War and Peace." Eight-part series appearing in *Ship's Monthly*, May–December 1990.

Seymour-Bell, Brigadier E. "The Cunard Tradition: A Proud Heritage." Address to the Newcomen Society in New London, CT, October 20, 1959.

Stairs, W. J. "A Merchant's Needs." Address delivered at Temperance Hall, Halifax, Nova Scotia, February 8, 1876.

Wood, William. "The Record Making-Royal William 1833." *Canadian Geographical Journal*, vol. 7, no. 2, 1933.

ACKNOWLEDGEMENTS

The task of writing a book is considerably enhanced and facilitated by the input of others. This has certainly been the case with *Steam Lion*, and I am most appreciative of the interest, encouragement and helpful advice many have so kindly given me with this work.

I am indebted to Nimbus Publishing, of Halifax, Nova Scotia, for undertaking to publish this long-overdue biography of one of Nova Scotia's most distinguished native sons. Special thanks to managing editor Sandra McIntyre and all the staff at Nimbus, whose teamwork has helped make this a most enjoyable experience.

Much of my research was conducted at Nova Scotia Archives and Records Management. To the entire archives staff, and in particular Virginia Clark, I extend my sincere thanks for the courteous, prompt, and professional service afforded to me as I laboured through the reference materials in this great resource centre.

One of the greatest pleasures I derive from being a Cunard historian is the people I meet along the way. Two in particular, both from the broader Cunard family, are deserving of special recognition. Hugh "Pete" Paton, of Charlottetown, Prince Edward Island, is a great-great-grandson of Samuel Cunard. Apart from being a good friend, Pete has been a staunch advocate and a great inspiration for this book. The same holds true for Ronald W. Warwick, commodore of the Cunard Line. The example he has set as master, author, and Cunard historian, as well as his insightful advice, have provided me with additional impetus with the writing of this biography.

Finally, no undertaking of this kind can succeed without the patience, understanding, and contribution of family. For what must have seemed to them to have been an eternity, my sons, Adam and Andrew, have tolerated my preoccupation with "the book." Both, much more technologically advanced than I, have helped when I have struggled with the computer to fashion the manuscript. Greatest praise, however, is directed to my wife, Judith, who has provided consistent and constant support for me in this endeavour.

IMAGE CREDITS

INDEX

For sales, editorial information, subsidiary rights information
or a catalog, please write or phone or e-mail
Brick Tower Press
1230 Park Avenue
New York, NY 10128, U.S.
Sales: 1-800-68-BRICK
Tel: 212-427-7139 Fax: 212-860-8852
www.BrickTowerPress.com
www.bookmanuscript.com
email: bricktower@aol.com.

For sales in the U.K. and Europe please contact our distributor,
Gazelle Book Services
Falcon House, Queens Square
Lancaster, LA1 1RN, U.K.
Tel: (01524) 68765 Fax: (01524) 63232
email: gazelle4go@aol.com.

For Australian and New Zealand sales please contact
INT Press Distribution Pyt. Ltd.
386 Mt. Alexander Road
Ascot Vale, VIC 3032, Australia
Tel: 61-3-9326 2416 Fax: 61-3-9326 2413
email: sales@intpress.com.au.